WILLIAM A. MAGUIRE
Captain, (Ch C), U. S. N.

THE CAPTAIN WEARS A CROSS

By

William A. Maguire

Captain (Ch C), U. S. N.
Staff, Commanding General,
Fleet Marine Force, San Diego Area

❧

JB
M276M

NEW YORK
THE MACMILLAN COMPANY
1943

*To the chaplains of the armed forces
of the United Nations who have given
their lives for God and country.*

Foreword

THIS IS A BOOK about the men of our Navy written by a man who must know as many of them, and know them as well, as anyone who ever wore the Navy's blue. Chaplain Maguire has, as much as any man I have ever known, a talent which is rare—the talent of knowing other men, not superficially or carelessly or through a veil of personal preconception, but as they are. To the varied, exacting tasks of his profession, he brings deep sympathy for other men and wide tolerance of their human foibles.

I saw those qualities exemplified when Chaplain Maguire served under me when I commanded the Scouting Force of the United States Fleet. I saw it in his day by day contact with the officers and men of the Force, to all of whom—quite without regard to their religious convictions—he was a trusted friend. For, like all good priests, he was more than a priest. His conception of his duty as a chaplain only began with the discharge of his strictly priestly duties. I have no idea where it ended because I never saw its end.

Chaplain Maguire's new book reflects the qualities of its author. It also reflects, to the discerning reader, the spirit which makes the United States Navy the great fighting team it is proving itself to be as I write these words. This is a book of countless stories of Navy men and of the families of Navy men. It shows them in battle and at prayer, in their homes and in their quarters. It tells alike of apprentice seamen and of admirals, because Chaplain Maguire is interested in all kinds of men. It tells of Catholics and Protestants and Jews; of serene men and worried men; of heroic death in line of duty and of long lives devoted to that same duty. There are stories in this book of that grim day at Pearl Harbor, when the men of our Navy came back fighting from a cowardly, bitter blow. There are stories of the distant days of peace, and of the closer, harder days which have come since the Japs stealthily attacked our ships as they lay at anchor.

It is a casual, discursive book and it is almost all about men of the Navy. Those who read it, if they read thoughtfully, will discover much of what our Navy is. They will better understand the fighting spirit, the heroism and the fortitude of our men, already exemplified so often and so gloriously in this war and among the best assurances of the war's successful outcome. For the men of whom Chaplain Maguire writes are typical of our Navy. So is the officer who writes of them.

ADOLPHUS ANDREWS,
Vice Admiral, U. S. Navy,
Commander, Eastern Sea Frontier.

Contents

Introduction

At Pearl Harbor in the Fall of 1941, Lord Louis Mountbatten, Captain of the Royal Navy, delivered an important lecture to the ranking officers of the Pacific Fleet. The admirals, their staffs and all commanding officers present, assembled in the auditorium of the submarine base to hear the distinguished naval officer, later vice admiral and British chief of the commandos, tell of his battle experiences in the Eastern Mediterranean. At the end of his thrilling account of the battle of Crete in which he described how the German "Stukas" bombed and sank his destroyer, the beloved *Kelly*, he allowed that the life of a destroyer man is not always a merry one.

He told us then of a destroyer that returned recently to a Channel port after many weeks at sea. The skipper, anticipating orders to return momentarily to the battle area, expected to find fuel available and stores neatly piled on the dock. But, to his utter dismay, he discovered that the commissary department of the dock-yard had ignored the fact of his arrival. With a hot burst of temper, he sent for one of his more pugnacious junior officers and voiced his resentment. "Smithers, step ashore and tell those commissary people to bear a hand. You know what to say. Hurry, young man, and give 'em hell."

The young officer, elated with this chance to perform in the spotlight, rushed to a telephone and began, with gusto, to fire a broadside. "You blasted blokes! Don't you know we're at war? What have you done with our stores and fuel? Don't you realize we may get underway tonight? You'd better jolly well get the stuff down here, and no damn kidding."

A deep, stentorian voice stung his ear. "Young man, do you know that you're addressing Vice Admiral Sir Sidney Windsor Winkle-Weather Drake?"

The Junior Officer nervously replied, "No, Sir." Then quickly gaining control, he inquired, "But, Sir, do you know who this is?"

The testy Admiral shouted, "No, silly ass! Of course not."

The recipient of the good news, as he hung up the receiver, softly murmured, "Thank you, Sir. That's all I want to know." The auditorium rang with our applause.

With the smiling grace of a Sir Walter Raleigh, the future Chief of Combined Operations, who was obviously in a hurry to catch the afternoon clipper for a flight to San Francisco, waved a cheerful farewell and departed.

Recently I told this story to my friend, Chaplain Walter A. Mahler, while we were motoring to Casa de Anita, my home in the foothills beyond San Diego, California. We had both been ordered to proceed from Hawaii to San Diego for duty; he to the Marine Corps base and I to the naval training station. As we climbed the steep knoll to the hacienda, Father Walter remarked, "Mac, it looks as though your book 'Rig for Church' were doing quite well. A young Marine came to me today and said he liked it. It may become a best seller."

Stepping out of the car and affecting a "limey" accent, I replied, "Thank you, old top—that's all I want to know."

That same evening I broke out the typewriter, placed it

on a table near the fireplace where "Duffy," my fox ter-
rier, looked up at me in amazement, and began to write this
sequel to "Rig for Church."

THE CAPTAIN WEARS A CROSS

CHAPTER I

"0745—Rig for Church"

THE JAPANESE RAID on the fleet at Pearl Harbor on the morning of December 7, 1941, was the theme of the last chapter of my book "Rig for Church." The official censors were indulgent in permitting me to describe, however sketchily, the highlights of that tragedy. That chapter, called "December Seventh," told how the Japs surprised us a few minutes before eight o'clock in the morning; how my yeoman Joseph Workman and I saw death fall from the sky although at first we thought it was a sham attack by our own Army planes. The first planes we saw were dive-bombers which dove vertically over the ships moored at 10-10 dock. A diagram of the harbor found on the body of a Japanese aviator which I was permitted to see a few weeks later in the austere privacy of an admiral's office, proved that the enemy thought the fleet flagship, *Pennsylvania*, was at her usual berth there. She was actually in dry-dock a quarter of a mile away. A few of their bombs struck the *"Pennsy"* but caused unimportant damage. The Jap's picture was so accurate, however, it clearly showed that the raid was an "inside job."

The Sunday work-sheet of the *California* carried this item: "0745—Rig for Church." It implied that I was expected to arrive on board a little after eight o'clock,

1

hear confessions in my office until nine, and then offer Holy Mass on the forecastle.

The staff motor-boat came alongside the Officers' Club landing at the very moment a squadron of torpedo planes dove out of the sun, pulled out when about thirty feet above the bay, dropped their glistening steel killers in the "middle aisle" and struck the side of the *Oklahoma*. Not until we spied the red "Rising Sun" insignia on the fuselage of the third plane, did we realize they were Japanese. Had we left the dock a few seconds earlier, our boat would have been in their murderous course. But this thought did not come to me until days later. Standing there with my foot on the gunwale of the boat, I felt stunned and strangely sick. The only words that came were: "God help us—we're in it." Overhead, there was a sinister pall of smoke, and the explosions of bombs and torpedoes rent the air. The first torpedo which struck the *Oklahoma* caused a huge geyser to rise as high as the truck of the foremast. This was a bit too realistic for a sham battle.

The first wave of torpedo-planes carried out their mission. Believing there would be a lull, I ordered the coxswain to make the gangway of a destroyer which was moored to a newly built dock about thirty yards from the club landing. The crew of the boat, although mad as hornets, showed splendid self-control. Indignant and without show of fear, the bluejackets said what they thought of the Jap and his treachery. With clenched fists, they cried, "We'll make you so-and-sos pay for this."

The engineer of the boat remembered the details of that trip and our final run across the bay to the *California*. He made a shipmate gesture of kindness a year later when I was on a speaking tour of the Eastern States. It was on account of a song called, "Praise the Lord and Pass the Ammunition." Written by Frank Loesser of Hollywood, it was a catchy tune, and the lyric caught on immediately. This was due, perhaps, to the fact that it told of a chaplain at Pearl Harbor who, when the Japs came, ran from his altar, manned a gun and exclaimed, "Praise the Lord, etc., etc. I just got one of those so-and-sos." For some reason or other, they made me the hero of the song. I may tell more about that later on. Maybe I shall tell how the publishers, radio stations and the "gentlemen of the press" took me over the hurdles. It delighted me to get Dick Smith's letter. It reached me at the Union League Club in New York. My cousin, John P. Maguire, thoughtfully put me up there, for he probably knew that the publicity I was receiving would make living in a hotel rather difficult. The sailor's address at that time was: U.S.S.P.C.1192, Consolidated Shipbuilding Co., Morris Heights, New York City. Here is the letter:

DEAR CAPTAIN:

I see, according to the newspapers, that you may be in hot water on account of that popular song. If I may, Sir, I'm sure I can help you out as I was the engineer of the Bat For Staff duty motor boat. As you remember, we, the boat crew, stayed with you until the attack was over. If you need any help, don't hesitate to let me know. Good luck.

As ever,

RICHARD GORDON SMITH

Machinist's Mate second class, USN.

A few minutes after we boarded a destroyer, which was then under the command of Commander George Angus Sinclair, another squadron of torpedo-planes swooped down close to our port beam. By this time, our

gunners on topside were ready for them. They scored a
perfect bull's-eye on one of the enemy planes. It exploded
in mid-air; bits of wreckage covered the water near us.
With contempt for the menace of falling shrapnel, the
sailors in my charge were all for retrieving the pieces
for souvenirs to send to the folks at home.

In my original account of the Jap raid, I omitted,
for many reasons, a dramatic incident which took place
just prior to my leaving the destroyer. The officer-of-the-
deck had told me the ship was soon to get underway.
Staying on board would have meant being many days at
sea. It was evident that I was needed on board the *California*, for she had been torpedoed. Men were in need of
a priest.

From where I stood on the well-deck, I could see dimly
through the smoke many men swimming near the damaged *Oklahoma*, the *West Virginia* and the *Arizona*. Some
were climbing on rafts; others were being hauled into
motor launches, while still others bobbed like corks in the
wind-swept waters. I gave general absolution. Knowing
that the *Maryland's* motor launch was alongside the destroyer, I requested authority of the officer-of-the-deck to
organize a rescue party, using the *Maryland's* boat because the high free board of the staff boat would be im-
practicable for the job. Joe Workman, the faithful watch-
dog of my Mass kit, at a nod from me, automatically sped
down the ladder and transferred the kit to the fifty-footer.
At that moment, I spied a motor-boat heading through
the smoke toward the landing. I made out the abbreviation
"Cal" on the bow. Cupping my hands, I yelled with all
my strength, "What are your orders, coxswain?" Faintly
came the reply, "To pick up the Admiral, Sir." I had now
to make an important decision—and quickly.

Never had I been hung so securely on the horns of a dilemma, or given so little time to decide what it was best to do. High altitude bombers had just destroyed the great *Arizona*. A fourteen-inch shell used as an aerial bomb had found her magazines, killing hundreds. Smaller planes were still strafing the ships. I prayed God for guidance and made an estimate of the situation: Vice Admiral William S. Pye, my immediate superior, was second in command of the Fleet. He was needed on board his flagship. As a member of his staff, I naturally felt impelled to pick him up with my boat in case anything happened to the other one. Also, I decided that the *Maryland's* coxswain was quite capable of taking his launch to the spot where the swimmers were struggling. With the approval of the officer-of-the-deck, I followed that line of reasoning and said, "Let's go, gang." My lads hopped aboard the staff boat and we "made knots" to the club landing.

During the ensuing days, I found no time to check on the work of the *Maryland's* boat but I know the crew must have carried out their mission. On the following Wednesday, I was informed that a Mass kit had been washed up near the ramp of a plane hangar on Ford Island. Apparently the launch had run afoul of burning oil on the water. Some thoughtful sailor had tossed the kit over the side. My favorite purple vestments which the children of Chefoo, China, had made, and the altar linens also, were oil-soaked and ruined. But the chalice, crucifix, altar stone and candle-sticks were intact. They had again survived the vicissitudes of my twenty-five years of Navy service.

Our boat arrived first. The moment we made fast to the landing, I saw Admiral Pye and several members of his staff hurrying down the path. In a jiffy, all that we could carry jumped aboard and we sped "four bells and a jingle" over the white-caps to the *California*, which was moored at a Ford Island quay. Among those who found places in the after section of the boat was Captain A. E. Smith, Battle Force Operations Officer. He was opposite Admiral Pye, who sat on the starboard side, next to me. Where the Admiral was seated, he could view the wrecked battleships. The *Oklahoma* had turned completely over. The demolished *Arizona* was burning fiercely. The Admiral kept leaning over the side to catch a better sight of the debacle, which prompted Captain Smith to warn him of falling shrapnel. Smith probably does not remember that while he knelt on the deck near the Admiral discussing the details of a fleet sortie, he tore his handkerchief into bits and stuffed the pieces into his ears. He knew that the roar from the A-A guns would not be good for his ear-drums. His sensible precautions also gave me an idea: there was cotton in the locker of my room.

Four torpedoes had hit the port side of the *California*, giving the ship a heavy list. The quarterdeck of teak which was normally as clean and white as snow, was now black-ened with soot. It was like a huge stage where a strange pageant was unfolding. The actors followed a studied routine; each actor had been rehearsed in precisely what to do; they had not drilled "around the clock" day-after-day at sea in vain. Before going below to my room, I looked up toward the A-A batteries. They were firing at some planes.

I found cotton in my room and jammed bits of it into my ears. Then I took off the old raincoat which the duty officer asked me to wear to hide the gold shoulder marks and white uniform. He was in dungarees and rather felt that my immaculate "whites" could readily draw the enemy's fire. I reached up to a rack on the overhang and pulled down a life-jacket. My gas mask was in my room at the Pacific Club. A bluejacket handed me one when I joined a group of men who were at their battle-stations in the port passageway.

The wardroom deck was covered with men. Most of them had been overcome by poisonous fumes that resulted from the exploding torpedoes. I found several more wounded men lying on the deck of the cabin of the Chief of Staff, Captain Harold C. Train. He was at his battle-station on the bridge. The men made a grim tableau lying there in the dark. But there was not a whimper from them. When I spoke to them and asked how they were doing, they smiled and invariably replied, "O.K., Sir." I heard many confessions and later gave general absolution to the ship's company.

While attending the wounded in the wardroom there was a foot of water in the officer's rooms on portside. Now and then I heard and felt an ominous c-r-u-n-c-h and thought the good ship would turn turtle as the *Oklahoma* had done a little while before. From time to time, believing there might be wounded up there in need of me, I climbed a ladder to the quarterdeck. It was difficult finding a place on the ladder, for a steady stream of men, each carrying a box of ammunition, climbed the steep ladder and then up another one to the guns on the boatdeck. Their faces, under a coat of oil and grease, were impassioned and stern. On reaching topside on one of these trips, I discovered that a ship's airplane had caught fire. It stood in its cradle aft on the port side. In the din of our roaring A-A batteries, I managed to attract the attention of the boatswain. He quickly assembled a working party of available sailors. But the ship's fire main had been destroyed by the torpedo hits. He thereupon ordered the men to push the big plane over the side.

While this "side-show" was being staged, I turned around as though someone had hailed me, and my eyes fell upon a seaman who was crouching beneath the platform of a three-inch sky-gun which was mounted near the starboard gangway. The lad frantically beckoned me to his side and I crouched near him on my knees. He yelled, "Hey, Father, how's to hear my confession?" He was not scared; an officer had ordered him to seek cover from falling shrapnel, for his gun at that moment was not being manned. The thought came to me then, although I tried to fight it off, "What will my other shipmates think—those passing by carrying ammunition boxes—seeing me on my knees. Will they think that I am pleading with the young sailor, 'Ease over, son, and give me a break?' " I said, "Of course, lad, but make it snappy, I've come without my tin hat." After giving the young fellow absolution, he thanked me and there was a smile on his Irish face. Then with a gleam in his blue eyes, he spat on his hands and exclaimed, "Now bring on them blasted Japs!"

I told that anecdote to Harvey Campbell, Executive Secretary of the Detroit Board of Commerce, in the fall of 1942, having been ordered to Detroit to give the principal Navy Day address. It impressed him. He said, with emotion, that it had not occurred to him till then that a chaplain under fire could give so much to the men with respect to mental freedom and fitness to fight. He visualized that boy spitting on his hands as having nothing on his conscience to worry about; he was certain his receiving the Sacrament had placed him on friendly terms with God. The lad was now free to carry on as a fighter for a sacred cause. Without doubt, this is the highest form of morale. It is fostering morale of this sort that keeps the Navy priest busy hearing confessions and giving Holy Communion to young men on the threshold of death.

This incident, so important in the life of that young bluejacket, exemplified the true mission of the chaplain in battle. In a radio broadcast I gave in New York last November on the Columbia System's "Church of the Air," I said, "The chaplain has but one weapon. He does not, he may not, man a gun. His fight is against the powers of darkness; his weapon is gold-embroidered on his sleeve or his shoulder marks. It is the saving cross of Jesus Christ."

Leaving the wardroom after a visit to the wounded, I heard a young officer sharply give the fateful order, "Abandon ship." His eyes gleamed. I felt then that there must be real danger of the ship's capsizing. I felt another c-r-u-n-c-h and a further list to port. Those of us who were free and able to do so, helped the wounded up the ladders to topside. The gallery-deck was ablaze. Ship's boats were alongside the quay to which the ship was moored and seemed to tug at the leash, aiming to get underway for the trip to the air station dispensary about a quarter of a mile away. The ship's first lieutenant, Commander Little, suggested that I take charge of one of the boats. It was a motor whaleboat and was about to shove off when I got aboard. Hundreds of men were on the quay and lowering themselves into the water for a swim to the beach. It was our own "little Dunkirk." The water in the bay was now covered with black, thick oil. Jap planes were still operating over Pearl Harbor, and I felt as I stood in the stern near the coxswain that this was a routine that any Hollywood director would have been proud to handle.

On our return to the ship, we made a path slowly through a great swarm of swimming men. Some in life-jackets waved to us as they leisurely swam past. Others, making headway without artificial aid, yelled, "This is duck soup." Maybe that was a sly reference to the thick oil on the water. We picked up another load at the quay and sped to the dock near the dispensary. On our third return, we ran into a barrier of burning oil and we discreetly made a left turn and escaped by beaching the boat. I waded through the muck and stood on the shore for a moment trying to figure out what to do next. From there, it appeared to me that all the wounded had been evacuated. A large group of men, who had swum from the ship, stood near me. They were blackened with oil. Some, with slight burns, were in pain. A Marine officer, driving a station-wagon, came up and offered to take the wounded to the dispensary. He made several trips, and each time he came to the dock I realized how much I was needed there.

CHAPTER II

"Put That Guy Up Here"

THE AIR STATION ferry boat, camouflaged to look like a field of wind-swept hay stacks, had its terminus at a point where our *California* refugees reached the shore. While I stood on the beach wondering whether all our wounded had been taken off, orders came for our men to return to the ship. They piled aboard the ferry in good spirits and seemed glad for the chance to get back to their posts. Among those who boarded the ferry, I found a few who were disabled. They were game and anxious to get back to the ship. I managed to get them ashore again and into the Marine officer's station-wagon.

Word was then passed, "Flag personnel report to the submarine base." Staff yeomen and others quickly jumped into a boat which was moored at the dock. Admiral Pye and most of his staff had already arrived at the submarine base where the Commander-in-Chief, Pacific Fleet, had his office. Among the flag people in the boat were my two yeomen. They were carrying out their orders but they seemed pleased when I spied them and signaled them with a wave of my hand to hop ashore and join me. They thought I had gone to the submarine base. It certainly felt good to have these fellows again with me; I needed them.

I asked Joe Workman where he had gone after we arrived at the club landing to pick up Admiral Pye. He said, "Well, Sir, I figured you'd want Red Durbin, and I had a hunch he was still at home. So I hopped into the car and drove to town to fetch him. I took a long chance as I didn't have a driver's license, but I kinda thought you wouldn't mind." I complimented Joe on his initiative. He had found Red standing on the porch of his little home bidding "so long" to Iris, his lovely wife. Joe added that the tall red-head from Oklahoma then manned the wheel and made a "full power" run to Pearl Harbor. Arriving at the Yard, they thoughtfully turned the car over to an improvised ambulance corps and told them to use it for carrying wounded to the hospital. Having taken care of that little detail and dodged the bullets of a Jap who strafed Merry Point landing, they set out "looking for the boss."

As we hurried from the ferry landing to the dispensary, we discovered that the starboard side of the *California* was still ablaze. Fire tugs played streams of water upon the boatdeck. The whole of battleship row had become a great inferno. Black clouds of smoke arose from where the destroyers *Cassin* and *Downes* had been bombed. Names of many chaplains came to my mind. I wondered whether the *Pennsylvania* had been destroyed. My old friend, Stanton Salisbury, was her chaplain. Not knowing the facts, I worried about Father Aloysius Schmitt, whose ship the *Oklahoma* had turned turtle, and I feared for chaplain Thomas Kirkpatrick, whose *Arizona* was a complete wreck. Later that day I was informed that both these chaplains had been killed. Salisbury, thank God, was safe.

When I looked up toward the gun platforms of the *California's* A-A batteries, I thought of Ensign Philip Haring. He was in command of many gunners up there. Phil and I had been shipmates for more than a year. He

was a graduate of Harvard and had joined the Naval
Reserve in the spring of 1940. Phil was an officer of unusual intelligence and spirit. I enjoyed many interesting
talks with him in my room. It was no surprise to me when
I learned later that he and his men had stuck to their guns
until the heat from the fires which had started below drove
them away.

I recall an evening the summer before in the home of
Commander John Kangeter. His wife "Tommy" and their
daughters, Peggy and Jean, were there.We were sitting on
the lanai of their hillside home, which commands a view of
Diamond Head and the lights of Honolulu, when Phil
Haring arrived. As was his custom, he was intent on discussing a matter of importance with me. We went to the
patio, where I learned that he had conceived some new
ideas for the shore entertainment of the men of his division.
It struck me as rather amusing at first that Phil, being on
liberty, should be so serious about it. But the happiness
of his men meant much to him and his ideas were good.
The bluejackets had a high regard for Phil. They saw in
him an officer and gentleman of distinction. They felt
that he considered their welfare his chief interest.

When we got to the dispensary, I found many dead and
dying. Doctor Arnold of Long Beach, California, was in
charge. He took me to a window and pointed to where a
Jap bomb had exploded exactly in the center of the square
patio. It made a large crater. A landscape architect could
not have been more accurate. It had injured no one. This
was the only piece of luck the Navy enjoyed on December
7th.

Having attended the wounded there, I went to the big
Marine barracks, where the overflow of wounded were

being placed on mess tables. I witnessed many acts of charity in that hall of pain. When a wounded bluejacket, badly shocked and burned, would notice a shipmate being carried in seemingly worse off than himself, he would say, "Take me down—put that guy up here—he needs it more than I do." Other men, leaning on the shoulders of their shipmates, exclaimed, "I'm okeh now, take me back to my ship—take me back to my gun."

Among the men, wet and black with oil, who grouped in the open spaces of the mess hall, I noticed a young blue-jacket who stood out from the rest. Most of the men were holding blankets tightly about their shoulders. This lad was wearing a uniform that was scarcely ever seen in tropical Pearl Harbor. It was a blue blouse with four gold stripes and a star on each sleeve. Surmounting several rows of campaign ribbons over the breast pocket were the gold wings of a naval aviator. The young sailor lifted his arm, gazed upon the four gold stripes and then looked down studying the ribbons and the wings. His young face was a picture of utter bewilderment. He seemed to say to himself, "How can they do this: promote me from seaman second class to captain over-night?" He did not realize at the time, nor did I, that some thoughtful fellow had raided the officers' quarters of the air station for clothing. Some one had tossed him the No. 1 blouse of Rear Admiral Patrick J. J. Bellinger. My friend, the distinguished aviator, who was then a rear admiral, had not got around to changing the stripes on his blue uniform. I had last seen Admiral Bellinger representing the Commander-in-Chief at the civic dinner given in honor of the newly arrived Bishop of Honolulu, the Most Reverend James Sweeney. On that occasion, the Admiral wore a white blouse.

I have since thought that the young bluejacket sym-

bolized at that moment the bewilderment of the 130,000,-
000 Americans on the mainland, "How can they do this to
us?"

Our patients had been given tags which indicated the
degree of their injuries. The most seriously wounded were
to be sent to the main hospital, the others to the newly
built mobile hospital near Aiea. I stayed with the wounded
on the ferry in order to assist in directing the trucks
when we arrived at Merry Point Landing.

While on a tour of the ferry boat, I discovered Chaplain
Raymond Hohenstein, the Lutheran chaplain who had
been assigned to the *California* in the summer when I was
ordered to serve exclusively on the staff of Commander
Battle Force as fleet chaplain. Ray was at his battle-
station when one of the exploding torpedoes filled the
compartment with deadly fumes. Sailors had carried him
to topside. He still looked a bit shaky.

The wounded were thus evacuated from Ford Island
by sunset. It occurred to me then that I should report my
activities to the Chief-of-Staff, Captain Harold C. Train.
It required half an hour or more to find my car. I remembered that Joe Workman had earlier told me that the
car had become an ambulance. While we were making a
tour of the big parking lot, a woman of the Red Cross
Motor Corps picked us up and patiently drove us around
the navy yard until we found my car parked near the
hospital.

Pearl Harbor was a scene of desolation. Battleship Row
was a sight to break a sailor's heart. The quarterdeck of
the *California* was awash. The *Arizona* was fiercely burning—fire tugs were pumping streams of water into the
open hatches, but the Stars and Stripes were still flying
at the mastheads of all our wounded ships. The men who

had lost their seagoing homes said little, for they were heart-sick; but there was fight in their eyes. They longed for another chance to come to grips with the Japs.

CHAPTER III

Blue Monday

WHETHER IT WAS DUE to pure luck or the advice of the Admiral's weather prophet, the Japs raided Pearl Harbor on Sunday, December 7th. It is well for them they did. Had they waited twenty-four hours, they would have missed the target, for on Monday, rain fell in torrents. It was certainly Blue Monday. When I first left the Pacific Club, Monday was worse than blue, for Honolulu's wartime blackout required the eyes of a cat to drive through the streets. I managed to reach the Cathedral of Our Lady of Peace and offer Holy Mass at 0700 in spite of the murky going. It was a Holy Day of obligation but I realized that the chaotic conditions in the navy yard would defeat any chance of mustering a congregation of sailors.

After Mass, Durbin drove me to Pearl Harbor. As we gingerly motored in the downpour over the slippery highway, my yeoman remarked, "Those monkeys were sure smart to pick Sunday." Many wrecked cars lay in the ditch beside the highway—victims of the blackout.

My plan was to visit outlying places in quest of seriously wounded. Our first stop was the new mobile hospital in the hills beyond Aiea. A group of Navy doctors and corpsmen had recently arrived from the mainland to build the unit. From all I could casually learn, they had brought the

17

"pieces" with them, so all they had to do was to put them together and make them fit. When we arrived, we found rows of steel huts standing in a sea of mud. But everything inside was shipshape. To my happy surprise, I discovered that my old friend, Dr. Chambers, a captain in the Medical Corps, was in command. He quickly told me there was no one critically ill and that the only things his patients needed were cigarettes, toilet articles and clothing. They had arrived the night before wrapped only in service blankets. It was a simple matter to drive a few miles to the canteen of the submarine base and pick up what was needed. We found a group of sailors standing at the counter waiting their turn to buy. When they learned that we were shopping for the wounded, they cheerfully shouted, "Gangway for the Chaplain—he's buyin' stuff for the wounded." One of the salesmen behind the counter insisted on carrying the heavy case of cigarettes to the car, which was parked about a city block from the canteen. Red Durbin protested, but the lad, a Filipino, insisted, "I want to carry it—it's an honor." I telephoned the Red Cross office in Honolulu. They promised to deliver shirts and dungarees to Dr. Chambers.

Our next call was at the plantation hospital in the town of Aiea. We found about forty men there, most of whom were bed patients. Chaplain Hohenstein was there, but he was well enough to help the doctors and nurses by taking the case histories of the bluejackets. We again drove to the submarine base for another load of cigarettes and toilet gear.

In the afternoon, we motored to the Marine air base at Ewa, another plantation town about fifteen miles from the navy yard. It occurred to me there might be seriously wounded out there in need of the Sacraments. The Marines of Ewa were a detachment of the fleet, and this gave me an added sense of pastoral responsibility. For several months, when the *California* was at sea, I had driven there on Sunday mornings and offered Mass in the mess hall, a long narrow room separated from the hot galley by a wire partition. The temperature was not unlike that of a Turkish bath.

On several occasions, Mrs. Edna B. Lawson of Honolulu came with me. For many years, she had been an important personage in Hawaii. She came to the Islands over twenty years ago to teach in the secondary schools. Her dramatic clubs were famous. When I first met the beloved "Edna B.," she was, in addition to being society editor and dramatic critic of the *Honolulu Advertiser*, the president of the Community Theatre. My duties often required me to attend meetings and to address the members of the Community Theatre about the entertainments which they generously gave the men of the fleet. They always invited our sailors to the dress rehearsals of the Broadway hits which they so capably presented.

Edna B. was fascinated by the primitive setting for Holy Mass at the Marine base. While I was hearing confessions, she sat in the car and chatted with the "leathernecks" who passed by on their way to the improvised chapel. She had a great affection for the men of the service—and the Marines liked Edna B. They inquired for her whenever she failed to appear at Sunday Mass.

I shall always be grateful to Mrs. Lawson for her advice and encouragement when I was preparing "Rig for Church" for the publishers. She came many times to the club in the fall of 1941 and had dinner with Father Tom Odlum and me. After dinner, we sat on the lanai of my cottage and worked over chapters that needed her professional touch. Edna B. had received her early education at St. Mary's College of Notre Dame, Indiana. About the time I first met her, St. Mary's gave her an honorary degree of Bachelor of Arts. This evoked happy memories of her school days and resulted in our learning much about her friend, Sister Madaleva, the distinguished poet, who is now president of the college.

I last saw Edna B. on Christmas day, 1941, when I stopped off at the Alexander Young Hotel to bid her a hasty farewell. She had been summoned on short notice to go aboard a transport about to sail to the mainland. I managed to have a short talk with her but I had to hurry to a radio studio where I gave a Christmas broadcast and then made a quick run to the hilltop home of the Kangeters for Christmas dinner. These dear friends of the Hawaiian days always made me feel that they had adopted me. I could not have felt more perfectly at home anywhere.

Less than a year before the Japs came, the Marine Aviation Unit was ordered to establish a base at Ewa on the fringe of a large sugar plantation. In the beginning, the only building was a small bungalow which the commanding officer and his executive used as headquarters. All hands lived in tents. Later on, a few shacks were built, including one for an officers' mess and another serving as a little beer garden for the men. Their first skipper was my old friend of the early twenties, Colonel Lewie G. Merritt, U.S.M.C. A few weeks before the Jap "blitz," Lewie was detached with orders to fly around the world inspecting bases and observing battle activities of the British Royal Air Force. His successor was another old shipmate, Colonel Claude A. "Sheriff" Larkin, U.S.M.C. We first met on board the transport *Chaumont* in Panama in 1926.

I found "Sheriff" in his office. He looked a bit down-hearted, but he generously offered to show me around. As we walked to the airfield, he remarked, "You're going to see something, Padre."

Parked in a huge circle were forty or more wrecks of the once proud squadron of dive-bombers. The first to catch my attention was the plane Colonel Merritt and I had used on the flight a few months before over the volcano of Mona Loa on the Big Island. The plane had been completely destroyed by bombs and incendiaries. The Japs had dived to the airfield while the Marines were at breakfast and worked over the area for an hour with machine guns and bombs. A wounded Marine, whom I later met in the hospital, told me how he and his buddies rushed out of the mess hall under fire and manned machine guns. But the Japs had too good a head start. He told of the heroism of one of the men. This leatherneck was in his plane doing the chores of early morning when the Japs dove out of the sun. Single handed, he fought with the gun he was cleaning. He was probably the first American to fire on the enemy in World War II. It may have been he who knocked down the Jap flier whose wrecked plane I saw that Monday afternoon. When the lone gunner's ammunition ran low, his comrades rushed out from the tent hangar with more. One of the men who handed up the ammunition to him was killed. The Marine in the plane fought in his exposed position until he was seriously wounded.

Ewa was the training base of the Marine aviators who later made imperishable history at Wake Island and Midway. From top to bottom, they were the best military outfit I have ever had the honor to serve.

Colonel Larkin, U.S.M.C. told of an incident during the attack which proved how well informed the enemy was regarding the location and organization of our forces on Oahu. As we strolled over the airfield where I picked up empty cartridges of various sizes and noted the lines cut in the ground which indicated how low the planes had flown, the Colonel said that one of the Jap fliers chose as his target the little cottage where the commanding officer and his second in command had their offices. The Jap, knowing that it was the custom of Colonel Lewie Merritt to look over his paper-work at eight o'clock on Sunday morning, had flown low and fired his machine gun at the office windows of the little house. He had not learned that Merritt was by that time in Singapore. Only a former employee at the Base could have conceived such an idea. It is not unlikely that he was an alumnus of the University of Hawaii.

On the return trip to Honolulu, it was a bit startling to see steel-helmeted, armed Japanese-Americans guarding bridges and other places of importance. They were members of the Hawaiian territorial guard. No one doubted their loyalty, but it made you feel rather uneasy. A story went the rounds of an American soldier who came to Honolulu in the first transport that arrived after the Pearl Harbor raid. Descending the gangway, he saw several slant-eyed soldiers on the pier and yelled back to his buddies on deck, "My God, we're too late!"

We dined early that winter because the Japanese servants at the Pacific Club were required to be in their homes before the blackout began, which was a little before six o'clock. One of the means of enforcing the blackout was to authorize the soldiery and the amateur warriors (high school boys) to "shoot out the lights" in houses and motor cars. It was certainly not a happy expedient, as I soon learned, and expensively.

Father Tom Odlum and I were about to leave the dining room one evening when a Japanese waiter told me that someone was wrecking my apartment in cottage #4. Hurrying to the lawn, I discovered a group of club members excitedly asking, "What's going on in the Padre's apartment? Hell's broken loose."

Someone inquired, "Did you have your light on?"

I was sure I had switched it off. Just then a bandy-legged soldier, with the grim look of a samurai, crashed open the screen door of the lanai and looking straight ahead, with his rifle at the hip, strode haughtily toward the Queen Emma Street gate. Although it was only 5:45 and not dark, this militia man had seen a light in my bathroom and fired a bullet through the bulb. Then he proceeded to break all the windows, crawled into my bedroom, knocked things about, and then took his martial leave. The club vehemently protested, and it worked. A few days later, the Army forbade "shooting out the lights." My first brush with the blackout set me back fifty bucks.

CHAPTER IV

"Don't Bother About Me"

My DUTIES AS Pacific Fleet chaplain, after the Japanese raid on Pearl Harbor, had so much to do with casualties that it was difficult to assume an unsentimental or professional attitude. When dealing with bereavement and sorrow, it was hardly wise to become too sorrowful myself especially when arrangements had to be made and details carefully handled. But I found it particularly difficult to receive stoically the news of the death of Ensign Herbert C. Jones, a shipmate of the *California*. He was a hero who exemplified the text of Holy Writ: "Greater love hath no man than this, that a man lay down his life for his friends."

When I heard of Herbert's death, I motored to Waikiki to express my sympathy to Joanne, his brave young widow. On the way, my mind persistently revived the happy scene of their wedding at which I officiated in Honolulu the summer of 1941. It was an especially happy occasion, a simple wedding to which only Herbert's young shipmates, Captain and Mrs. F. C. Sherman, and a few civilian friends were invited. Mrs. Jones, Herbert's mother, had come from the mainland for the occasion. But she came alone, for his father, a naval officer, Captain Herbert A. Jones, retired on account of physical disability, was too ill at the time for the long journey. A chaplain, over a quarter of a century, performs many marriages, but among them are a few which seem to attach him in an intimate manner to the family circle. I felt that way about the marriage of Joanne and Herbert; and that afternoon, when I arrived at the hotel, I realized that this was a duty-call close to my heart.

The last time I had spoken with Herbert Jones was an evening in November, 1941, when the *California* lay at anchor off Long Beach, California. We had sailing orders to leave the following morning for Hawaii. In the motorboat on the run to the ship, the young ensign was in high spirits. He had seen his family in Coronado and now he was about to rejoin his beloved Joanne in Honolulu. I have forgotten what he said on that short trip, but he kept us laughing all the way to the ship. Herbert was a handsome fellow and I cannot recall ever seeing him when his good nature was not revealed in his smiling eyes.

At an early age, this boy was already steeped in the traditions and customs of the Navy—he had lived at the Naval Academy, Annapolis, for six years of his life while his father did duty as an instructor in mathematics and navigation. He had travelled with his family at home and abroad, sometimes sailing on board his father's command. He wanted to follow in his father's footsteps and enter the Naval Academy but no congressman or senator of his district would give him an appointment and in the end he entered a university. As soon as war became imminent, Herbert joined the first class of college men chosen to undergo special training for commissioning as ensigns, U.S. Naval Reserve. He was ordered to the Reserve Officers' Training School in New York City and on graduation, the Bureau assigned him to the *California*, the flagship of the Battle Force.

Arriving at the hotel, I found Joanne in the apartment of Mrs. J. W. Bunkley, the wife of the commanding officer of the ship. No one could have been more sweetly resigned to sorrow. Joanne had heard how heroically Herbert had died during the battle and this may have helped her to bravely conceal her emotions.

The following morning, they carried Herbert's body to the Church of St. Augustine where I offered a Requiem Mass. That afternoon, Joanne boarded a clipper and flew to her parents' home in California.

When my old friend, Commander John Ford, the famous director of motion pictures, came to Honolulu, his first thought was to visit the grave of Herbert Jones. One afternoon, after John had made preliminary arrangements for making the picture called "December the Seventh," he rounded up his cameramen, had me order a basket of flowers, and we all drove out to the Halawa Cemetery which is on a hill overlooking Pearl Harbor. With Chief Boatswain Jack Pennick who, for many years had been John Ford's assistant at Hollywood, we posed for pictures near the young hero's grave. But the scene that would have made the best memento for the Jones family was not photographed. After the cameramen had left and we were about to leave the cemetery, Ford and Pennick walked slowly back to the grave, knelt on the grass, and for several minutes prayed for the repose of Herbert's soul. It deeply impressed me. I wish I now had a picture of that scene, because it was the best that John Ford ever directed.

Herbert's bravery was to my mind one of the most outstanding examples of deliberate self-sacrifice yet recorded. The real story of his heroism I know from accounts of those who investigated his death and from reports of eye-witnesses.

At Pearl Harbor, Sunday December 7, 1941, he came

on deck at 7:45 A.M., ready to relieve the officer of the deck. A few moments later, the Japanese planes swooped out of the skies. A torpedo struck the side of the *California*, and the explosion shook that great ship from stem to stern; oil flowed from a storage tank covering a lower deck; fires started; men rushed on deck from below and black forbidding smoke belched out of the hatch. Someone cried, "There's a man knocked out, layin' in oil below." Herbert rushed into the smoke-filled compartment, rescued the man, then he collapsed when he reached the deck. He was soon revived and though still weak from the fumes, he ran forward to his 5″ anti-aircraft battery. Several rounds of ammunition for each gun had been previously laid out on deck for emergency action—the rest of the ammunition was stowed as usual in the magazines deep in the bowels of the ship.

When the next Jap planes came in a murderous wave, they were met with anti-aircraft fire but no new supply of ammunition was coming to the guns. The batteries continued to fire as long as the emergency ammunition lasted and then all were silenced. It was found that the ammunition hoist had been damaged by the first torpedo to strike the ship. The magazines could be reached only through smoke-filled and blazing compartments. Herbert asked for volunteers, quickly organized his party and formed a line from deck to magazine. They passed ammunition by hand to the anti-aircraft guns. Another wave of Jap planes swept over the *California* and a torpedo struck her side. A bomb penetrated the upper deck and exploded near Herbert. Smoke and fire filled the shattered compartment. Men, gassed and wounded, got to the deck above. Two, seeing Herbert lying mortally wounded, went to his assistance. As his men tried to carry him to safety, he bravely shouted, "Don't bother about me. Save yourselves before the magazines blow up."

President Roosevelt awarded Herbert posthumously the Congressional Medal of Honor, the highest award this nation can bestow on its heroes. A part of the citation read, "for conspicuous devotion to duty, extraordinary courage, and complete disregard of his own life above and beyond the call of duty."

The memory of this young reservist will be perpetuated in the Navy when the U.S.S. *Herbert C. Jones*, an escort destroyer, joins the fleet. Captain and Mrs. Herbert A. Jones and Joanne, Herbert's young bride, in January, 1943, journeyed to Orange, Texas, where Joanne christened the warship. A ship, too, needs a soul, and my prayer is that the officers and crew of this vessel build into its sturdy frame the spirit and soul of my young friend, Ensign Herbert C. Jones, U.S.N.R.

I recently obtained from the parents of Ensign Jones a copy of an address of the Secretary of the Navy, the Hon. Frank Knox, to the eleventh graduating class of U.S. Naval Reserve Ensigns in New York City, March 31st, 1943. He said, in part:

"I am going to talk to you about two men named Jones, two officers in the Navy—the American Navy. You guessed the first one was John Paul, of course, and I would like to say to you that in all the years that have passed since John Paul Jones voiced his definition of a naval officer, the American Navy has never included a finer or more honorable spirit than his. And I would like to give to you, out of his rich experience and his tremendous accomplishments, his definition of what constitutes a naval officer. Possibly I may be repeating some of these lines to some of you but indeed they are well worthy of the emphasis that comes from repetition. Speaking of qualifications of a naval officer, John Paul Jones said:

" 'It is by no means enough that an officer of the Navy should be a capable mariner. He must be that, of course, but also a great deal more. He should be, as well, a gentleman of liberal education and refined manners, punctilious courtesy, and the nicest sense of personal honor.

" '. . . . The naval officer aboard ship and in relation to those under his command should be the soul of tact, patience, justice, firmness and charity. No meritorious act of a subordinate should escape his attention or be left to pass without its reward, even if the reward be only one word of approval. Conversely, he should not be blind to a single fault in any subordinate, though, at the same time, he should be quick and unfailing to distinguish error from malice, thoughtlessness from incompetency and well-meant shortcoming from heedless or stupid blunder.'

"We haven't improved on that definition in all the years that have gone by since, and I love to think—and I do think—that the fine spirit inculcated in the American Navy in the very beginning by John Paul Jones has been carried along through the years and generations by his successors. And may I take this opportunity to pay my tribute to the commissioned officers of the Regular Navy with whom I have served for the past two and a half years —as splendid a group of officers as it has ever been my good fortune to meet. . . .

"Now for the other gentleman. I came down here when the first class was about to graduate from this school. And among the members of that class which graduated at that time was another Jones—Herbert C. Jones. He was an officer who came into the service after the war began, shortly before we got into it. Graduated from this class, sent to duty at sea, and when the fateful day of December 7th came, he was junior officer on one of our ships of the fleet at Pearl Harbor. Due to the fact that the ammunition hoist had broken down, he had gone below to superintend the handling of ammunition by hand in order to supply the guns that were returning the attack of the Japanese. A shell penetrated the interior of the ship, set it aflame, fatally wounded young Jones, and two of his crew tried to rescue him although the compartment was blazing. He ordered them on deck and met his fate there in that lower compartment alone. And his family cherish today the highest decoration the American Government can bestow —the Congressional Medal of Honor awarded posthumously.

"That boy was just such a boy as you who came through the indoctrination of this school, who absorbed from his associates and superiors in the Navy that fine, high spirit of sacrifice and who met his hour like an American. I have no doubt that many of the men who listen to me today will find themselves in battle. You would do well to remember young Herbert C. Jones and the spirit with which he met his test."

One evening in the fall of 1942, Herbert's parents and Joanne came to my home for dinner. On the mantelpiece in the living room, they saw a picture of my late father in a beautifully carved frame of jade. The frame was a present Joanne and Herbert gave me as a remembrance of their marriage in Hawaii. It is among my dearest treasures.

CHAPTER V

Reported Missing

ALTHOUGH I REQUESTED duty on board a combatant ship, the Commander-in-Chief decided that I should retain my office in Honolulu. For ten months the sign, "Fleet Chaplain, Pacific," stood on my desk in the reading room of the Army and Navy Y.M.C.A. The secretary in charge of that well-appointed oasis of hospitality and good cheer, Wesley Wilke, insisted that I take over the small reading room on the second floor for an office. The "Y" was a convenient place for the men to find me when they came to town on liberty. Many of our ships were still without chaplains. My friend "Wes" is one of the most successful "Y" secretaries I have known. He "savvies" the needs of the enlisted man and he is always ready to lend a chaplain a helping hand in his work for the welfare of the men.

My mission in Honolulu had undergone a complete change. As liaison officer between the fleet and the Mayor's Entertainment Committee, my job had been to coordinate entertainment activities for the men of the fleet. I now had duties that were certainly less enjoyable.

The Pearl Harbor casualty list which Rear Admiral Robert A. Theobald turned over to me soon after the Jap raid, included many unavoidable errors. Some men were listed as "missing" when we had reason to believe they were being cared for in homes near the shore of Pearl Harbor. Men had swum from their ships and, in a dazed condition, had wandered through the plantation fields and elsewhere. From time to time, I requested the local radio stations to broadcast something like this: "If there are wounded Navy men in your homes, unable to return to the navy yard, please 'phone the Fleet Chaplain, etc., etc." We located several men in this way. They were being sheltered in the homes of kind-hearted Hawaiians.

One afternoon in December, Eugene Burns of the Associated Press, came to my office for an interview. He won me over immediately by his forthright manner and his sincere desire to encourage the people on the mainland with accounts of the heroic deeds of our boys at Pearl Harbor. We saw eye-to-eye with respect to the importance of collecting stories about individual deeds beyond the ordinary call of duty and of publishing the accounts in the hero's home-town paper. I assured Burns that I would help him gather material in the hospital at Pearl Harbor which he would send by dispatch to bolster the morale on the home-front. It surprised me that evening to read in the Honolulu *Star-Bulletin*, a story mostly about myself. Burns quoted my words of praise for the men of the fleet. His story appeared the next day in over three hundred papers in the United States. I did not relish the attendant publicity but it did give the name of a person in Hawaii to whom bereaved mothers and wives could write. The next shipment of mail gave me a new and trying task. So many letters came that it was necessary to ask for additional clerical help. The efficient Lee Durbin became even more valuable to me. As a stenographer, he was not only a sprinter, but he had the endurance of a Gregg Rice of Notre Dame.

In the first pile of mail, I found a heart-breaking letter from a Mrs. Daley of Brooklyn. I can repeat it almost word-for-word.

DEAR FATHER:

The Navy Department has informed me that my son Jim has been reported missing at Pearl Harbor. I am a widow and Jim was my only child. He was a radioman first class. Jim was always a good boy. Please help a broken-hearted mother. Look for him. Maybe he is wandering in the hills. I can't believe he is dead.

I looked through the long casualty list, but the name "Daley" was not listed. I turned to Durbin and said, "Take a letter, Lee—here's a tough one."

The sympathetic red-head picked up his pad and softly replied, "Aye, aye, Sir."

Just then I heard a familiar voice. "Good morning, Father." I looked up at the cheerful face of Parker, chaplain on Daley's ship.

"Hello, Parker, you're just the man I want to see. Do you know Jim Daley, radioman 1st?"

"Very well," he replied. "I was talking to him less than an hour ago."

"Thank God! Read this." I handed him the letter, then added: "Before you give me the story, Chaplain, I'll get off a dispatch to Daley's mother." Then to my yeoman, "Durbin, take this down for Mrs. Daley. 'Your son Jim is hale and hearty.'" Then to my other yeoman, Joe Workman, "Take this to the cable office and chop chop." With a smile, Joe picked up his gas mask and fairly zoomed through the door.

Chaplain Parker told us that Jim Daley had just come

off watch when the Japs struck. He was standing on the dock chatting with a shipmate. After the second attack by torpedo-planes, a yard tug came near and the skipper, being short-handed, yelled to Daley and his friend to lend a hand. They promptly jumped aboard and spent five days at sea as deck-hands on the tug. When a muster was taken on board, they were reported among the "missing."

Several weeks later, Mrs. Daley wrote from Brooklyn that the cablegram was delivered the afternoon of the day she had called at the rectory to ask one of the Fathers to offer a Mass for her son Jim. On getting the good news, she hastened back and requested that it be a Mass of thanksgiving. Her joyous letter was indeed touching.

I rather believe that the most trying word in our language is that enigma, "missing." But it is encouraging to learn how many people in their strong faith in God's mercy refuse to believe the word means "lost." Hundreds of letters that reached me in Hawaii expressed this pathetic refusal to believe that the missing one, in answer to prayer, would not some day be reported alive. It was particularly tragic when letters came inquiring about "missing" men who had served in the battleship *Arizona*. Since it was impossible to recover and identify the bodies of so many who were killed in that ship, the only safe thing to do was to employ for a long time that unsatisfactory word, "missing."

Light broke occasionally through the clouds of gloom as in the case of the young Navy wife who one day came to my desk. Her husband, a petty officer, had been transferred from the *Arizona* to a cruiser. But there was a delay in sending his transfer papers to the cruiser. The man's name was still on the roster of the cruiser on the

morning of December 7th. When a check was made, they
reported him "missing." US M 587057

The sailor's wife who was painfully worried, began her
story by simply stating, "I have a telegram from the
Navy Department saying my husband is 'missing.' " I
gently asked the name of the ship. "He used to be on the
Arizona," she replied. My chin dropped. "But," she continued, "he wasn't on the *Arizona* on the 7th. He was on
a cruiser." And she named it. "I saw him last Wednesday.
And now they tell me he's missing. Has the cruiser been
sunk?" That stopped me. I had no news of my old ship in
which I had spent two and a half peaceful years. I begged
the young woman to be patient while I made inquiries. The
next day it was indeed gratifying to be able to erase the
ugly word "missing" from her troubled mind.

The permanent residents of Honolulu were quite as
painfully shocked as the Navy folk when the papers announced the loss of the heavy cruiser *Houston* in the battle
of the Java Sea. The flagship of the Asiatic Fleet had been
a unit in the Hawaiian Detachment long enough for the
ship's company to make many friends in Honolulu. For
a time Admiral Andrews flew his flag on the *Houston;*
he and his staff lived on board for two or three months.
She was a smart ship; her officers were kind to us and the
crew were splendid shipmates. They showed how proud
they were of their ship by keeping her always immaculately
clean. Her commanding officer then was Captain Jesse B.
Oldendorf; he is now an admiral. The executive officer
was Commander Alexander R. Early. One of the younger
officers was Lieutenant (jg) Harold S. Hamlin, Jr.

A few months prior to the departure of the *Houston*
from Pearl Harbor to become flagship of the Asiatic

Fleet, Hamlin married a member of a prominent Honolulu family.

One day after the outbreak of war, I was asked to call on Mrs. Hamlin. She had received word from the Navy Department that her husband was "missing." Realizing that the *Houston*, although previously damaged, had desperately fought a superior force to the end, I wondered, as I drove to Mrs. Hamlin's home, whether I should encourage the young wife to continue hoping for her husband's safety or help her to be resigned to what so many of us feared was the tragic truth. When I met her in the living room, I discovered at once that Mrs. Hamlin had built a strong barrier against believing that her "Hal" had not in some way escaped death by reaching the shore of some little island. She had studied maps of the area where the battle took place; and she felt confident that the enemy ships would pick up the *Houston* survivors. Her optimism was infectious. After listening to her defense of her brave decision not to give up hope and her spirited expression of faith in the mercy of God and the power of prayer, I agreed that the word "missing" should be interpreted the way she had chosen.

A year later, I received a V-mail letter from Mrs. Hamlin. Here it is:

DEAR FATHER MAGUIRE:

My hope and faith for Hal's safety was justified. My prayers have been answered, for two of Hal's shipmates have broadcast by transcription over Tokyo radio and said they saw Hal in April. Apparently he was not with them when they made the transcription, but he was safe in April. My thanksgiving began two weeks ago today—I am so thankful. My faith and hope now is renewed for the duration. I shall attempt to write although

I know not just where he is. I feel certain the Japanese are human enough to deliver mail. We have heard messages and transcriptions of six men and they spoke of at least nine others. That means we know of fifteen officers who are safe. My prayers continue as do my thanks. I was so certain I had every right to hope and I shall continue my faith for the duration.

Ever sincerely,

/s/ KATHLEEN HAMLIN

May God grant that these two courageous souls may be happily reunited after the war is won.

CHAPTER VI

Battle of the Bands

DRIVING A CAR on moonless nights in Honolulu was indeed a stunt. Only a faint blue light was permitted by law to glimmer in the lamps as a signal to approaching drivers of your presence in the street. Keeping the car off the sidewalks was a matter of sheer luck. A few days following the Jap "blitz," Father Tom Odlum and I undertook to reach the home of the John Kangeters. Soldiers and amateur police officers stopped us at every street corner and demanded that we show our passes. Driving through town was an achievement; but when I managed the steep private road that led from the highway to the Kangeter home on Pacific Heights, I felt there was something to brag about. Climbing the steps to the lanai, we found the house in total darkness. With a dimmed flashlight, we spied the doorbell button and wondered in the ghostly silence whether our friends were really there.

Mrs. "Tommy" Kangeter greeted us in the dark living room and led us on a devious course to the blacked-out dining room, where we found a large group of women and children. Tommy introduced them as refugees from the Army's Hickam Field. The Japs had bombed them from their quarters, and the charitable Tommy promptly offered them hospitality. She was in complete charge, for her husband, Commander John, was required by a new regulation to remain day and night at his post in the navy yard. But his versatile wife, in the manner of a jovial bosun's mate, ran the outfit with a deft but firm hand. Her only worry was a young Army junior who thought it amusing to get up in the dead of night and switch on the lights. This nine-year-old girl was able to keep her patient benefactress in nightly dithers.

Honolulu seriously respected the rules of the blackout. Even though the order "shoot out the lights" had gone by the board during the first week following the "blitz," the job of concealing the whereabouts of our homes from raiding Japs became the prime nuisance of our lives. War correspondents who came through Honolulu in December were amazed to find how "black" a city could be made after dark. They all said that the rules were far more rigid than in Berlin or London. Until we contrived schemes for ventilation by building little box-like affairs outside the windows, our rooms became stifling after a few minutes. We then turned out the lights, opened the windows and blamed Tokyo, as we chatted in the darkness.

At the Pacific Club during the days of middle December, we gathered in the evening in Elverton R. Champion's cottage to hear "Radio Tokyo" tell of the progress of the war. In those days, the news was not good whether it came from Tokyo or Washington. But Jap propaganda soon depressed us, and we sought comfort and cheer in the nonsense of Edgar Bergen's "Charlie McCarthy."

It was quite noticeable that the bluejackets and Marines at Pearl Harbor were deeply affected and depressed by the loss of 3,000 shipmates. This struck me forcibly every time I drove to the navy yard or when I looked into the faces of our men during their too few liberties in town.

I then felt it my duty to recommend that we hold a brief Memorial Service and combine the solemn payment of tribute to our honored dead with an appeal to our young sailors to "snap out of it, and get in there and pitch."

When the Secretary of the Navy, the Honorable Frank Knox, arrived by plane in early December, it seemed the appropriate time. My plan was to assemble the men on the ball field as a precaution against a possible air raid and hold there a brief Service. For some reason, the Admiral then in command of the fleet disapproved. It rankled in me for days until I learned that a "Battle of the Bands" was to be held the coming Sunday afternoon in the fleet boxing arena. This simple form of amusement was a program that called for competitive renditions by the few battleship bands still intact.

That Sunday afternoon, I arrived early and got the ear of Chief Boudreau, the master of ceremonies. My friends for many years, Joe Fisher and Sam Soboloff of the Welfare Department, were there and heartily approved of the idea.

Before the "battle," I mounted the stage and made a speech. "Shipmates, this 'Battle of the Bands' is a fine idea. I am sure the music will do you good. But I suggest that before we begin the contest, we give a prayerful thought to our shipmates who recently gave their lives in a real battle. I ask you to rise and offer a silent prayer for their eternal peace." At that moment a bugler, who stood in a far corner of the arena, softly sounded "taps."

I continued: "Shipmates, in our simple way we have paid honor to our departed friends. Let us now pray Almighty God that we may be inspired with the same spirit they had on December 7th. Let us keep our spirits high and carry on with all our heart and soul in this fight for victory." One of the bands then struck up the popular song, "God Bless America," and all hands sang with gusto.

That was Pearl Harbor's first Memorial Service. It was hardly adequate, but it was dignified. I shall always be glad it was done.

For months, our battleships were tombs of our heroic shipmates. Each afternoon, when bodies were recovered from the decks below, the chaplains of the 14th Naval District, Thornton Miller, Father Thomas Odlum and the Jewish chaplain, Cerf Straus, held services at the cemetery. Occasionally they invited me to conduct the Catholic service. My duties were such that I seldom found time to go to the cemetery.

When ships of task forces returned to Pearl Harbor after many weeks at sea, officers and men on topside came to attention and saluted their dead comrades as the ships slowly steamed past Battleship Row to their anchorages. Our men will never forget that experience. It gave them a sublime motive for their war-time life of self-abnegation.

CHAPTER VII

Lost in the Solomons

WHEN THE NAVY announced that the heavy cruiser *Astoria* was lost in a sea battle off Savo in the Solomons, it shocked me, because I knew her well. In 1935, Father Vincent J. Gorski had hurriedly left the *Astoria* at a Pacific port on dispatch orders to be my relief when the medico put me on the sick list at the training station in Newport, Rhode Island. Vince spoke in high praise of the ship and I remembered this in the spring of 1938, when I joined the staff of Vice Admiral Adolphus Andrews, Commander Scouting Force. The *Astoria* was in our outfit and had no chaplain. I went on board on many occasions and offered Sunday Mass in the roomy plane hangar.

In the fall of 1939, with Admiral Andrews in command, a fast, hard-striking collection of our latest models in destroyers, cruisers, patrol planes and the carrier, *Enterprise*, set sail for Hawaii and based at Pearl Harbor. It was known as the Hawaiian Detachment, and we naturally hooked up our destiny with Hitler's march into Poland, and thought it rather romantic. The "Hawdet" was a smart little fleet and her personnel were as peppy as rodeo cowboys. Maybe we felt that if there were to be action in the Pacific, we'd be the first to fight.

Each chaplain of "Hawdet" held two services on Sunday, the earlier one on board a ship other than his own.

I often chose the *Astoria* for my first Mass and became well acquainted with her crew.

It was one of my duties as force chaplain to confer with the skippers on welfare matters, and to call on the admirals who commanded the divisions. One morning, I went aboard the *Minneapolis* to talk over things with the commanding officer, Captain David I. Hendrick. We had been shipmates twenty years before in the *Idaho* when he was assistant engineering officer and lived in a room next to mine. The tall and witty "Dave" had not changed much, for he was never one to worry about things that never happened. At the end of my visit, when he courteously started to escort me to the gangway, I suddenly thought it was a good time to pay my repects to Rear Admiral Royal Ingersoll, the Division Commander. His ability as a strategist was well known in the Force, and I am sure no one was surprised when we later heard that he became Commander-in-Chief of the Atlantic Fleet and a four star admiral. When I entered his cabin, Admiral Ingersoll had his cap in hand, preparing to leave the ship to see the finish of the Battenberg Cup race. He invited me to go along in his barge and assured me that the crew of his flagship would win. I spent a pleasant hour chatting with him in the barge and I realized again how simple and human a distinguished admiral can be, and a cheerful loser, too. The oarsmen of the *Enterprise* beat the "*Minnie*" by three boat-lengths. I have forgotten how the *Astoria* finished, but I know they had a good crew.

Captain Richmond Kelly Turner then commanded the *Astoria*. He is now a rear admiral fighting the Japs somewhere in the South Pacific. When I first called on Captain

Turner, he showed sincere interest in the work of our chaplains and invited me to come frequently to his ship to offer Mass for his Catholic men. He had just brought the *Astoria* back from an important voyage to Japan when she carried the ashes of the Japanese ambassador to his home land.

My interest in the ship was increased when Father Walter A. Mahler became the *Astoria's* chaplain. He had done his sea-apprenticeship in the tender *Medusa* when the popular Captain Thomas J. Doyle, Jr. was in command. "Tee" Doyle I had known for years especially as the Annapolis roommate and life-long pal of my friend Captain Oliver O. "Scrappy" Kessing. Tee and Scrappy more closely approached the story-book ideal of the naval officer than any two of my acquaintances. They now hold important combat billets; and if imagination, aggressiveness, skill and sense of humor any longer count in warfare, they will keep the situation well in hand. A few days before Chaplain Mahler left the *Medusa*, we had lunch with the inimitable Tee Doyle in his cabin. He told us then that orders had come assigning him to command of the submarine base at Coco Solo in the Canal Zone. Captain Doyle is a submarine skipper of wide experience.

Although Father Mahler regretted leaving his old shipmates, he was like a boy with a report card of A's when he showed me his orders to the smart *Astoria*.

I saw a great deal of Father Mahler on board and ashore in those days but I always found it hard to get him to say much about the ship. Even before the Pearl Harbor raid, my friend interpreted rigidly the orders regarding "security." With respect to the sea employment of his ship, he was steadfast in keeping mum. As far as getting anything from him about the *Astoria's* doings at sea, he might just as well have been a landlubber living across the street.

One day, months before the "blitz," after an especially long absence from Pearl Harbor, he came to my cottage at the Pacific Club. I naturally asked, "Hey, where have you been all these months?"

"Oh," he replied, "you know—same old thing, cruisin' around."

"Very well," I answered, pretending to be annoyed, "if that's the way it is, let's skip it."

"Well, if you must know, I saw Mac."

This was too much. "Mac which? There is a limit, Walter, to this 'security' business."

Thereupon, he revealed that he had seen Father Francis J. McManus. I knew he was chaplain of the submarine force of the Asiatic Fleet, so the *Astoria* must have gone to Manila. It was an easy deduction.

The chance came, some weeks later, to get "square" with my secretive colleague. He brought two of his messmates, the jolly engineer officer, Lieutenant Commander John D. Hayes, and the more serious gunnery officer, Lieutenant William H. Truesdell, to the club for lunch. Afterward, we sat on my lanai for a chat. While we were discussing the relative merits of the local golf courses, I suddenly broke in with, "You fellows don't have to tell me where you have been. If I want to know anything about the *Astoria* and the interesting things you have been doing, I ask Father Mahler. He's the most talkative guy I know, especially regarding movements of the cruisers. You fellows had better do something about it."

They caught on at once but we had a lot of fun at the young padre's expense. Father Mahler was equal to the "rib."

When the *Astoria's* commanding officer, Captain Preston B. Haines, took sick a few weeks after the Jap raid, he was detached. "Pret" and I had been shipmates on the Asiatic station in 1930. He was then executive officer of the old coal burner *Pittsburgh* and I served six weeks on board her when she took the Governor General of the Philippines, the Hon. Dwight Davis, on a cruise to Siam and the Netherlands East Indies. We admired and liked Pret for the cheerful way he inspired the confidence and respect of his shipmates. From the stories Father Mahler told of his skipper, the *Astoria* had reason to lament his leaving. The Navy chose as Haines' relief the capable Captain Francis W. Scanland. I had known him in the late twenties when he was the battleship *Arkansas'* navigator. I shall always be grateful to Frank that he had the day's duty the cold December afternoon I reported when the ship was undergoing overhaul in the Philadelphia Navy Yard. He was genuinely hospitable in a quiet sort of way and I grew very fond of him on the cruise that winter in the Caribbean. When the Hawaiian Detachment arrived, Frank had command of the Pearl Harbor submarine base.

Captain Scanland came from the "cheer-up" ship, *Nevada,* which he commanded before and after December the seventh. I knew the *Nevada's* officers and some of the enlisted men, having, as a passenger, made a trip aboard her from Long Beach, California, to Hawaii in the spring of 1941. Rear Admiral Francis W. Rockwell, who was then a captain, was skipper. We had served together in

1934 in the battleship *Mississippi;* he was the executive officer and one of the best liked officers the "*Missy*" ever had. He is tall and slender and gentle as a bear cub when things are going well. His classmates at Annapolis dubbed him "Skinney"—and it stuck. At the outbreak of the war with Japan, Admiral Rockwell was commandant of the 16th Naval District with headquarters at Cavite, P. I. The Navy decorated him for heroism after his memorable escape from Corregidor with General Douglas MacArthur in one of Lieutenant Commander J. D. Bulkeley's "expendables."

I recall a pleasant dinner party one night at sea in Captain Rockwell's cabin. Father Raymond Drinan, the ship's chaplain and the famous news photographer, Al Brick, were among the guests. Brick had been the hero of many a photographic news-scoop in the past but I think Al's best job was being on the spot with his camera when the Japs attacked our fleet at Pearl Harbor. His pictures were little short of marvelous.

On the morning of the 7th of December, on orders to put to sea, the *Nevada* got under way and was nearing the entrance to the channel when a Jap torpedo opened a big hole in her port side. They managed to beach her across from Hospital Point where she later commanded a view of the ships that left the channel for the open sea. The fine old *Nevada*, before she could again join the battle line, was doomed to many months of overhaul.

Father Mahler told me of the *Astoria's* first departure under command of her new skipper. In company with other units of the task force, the cruiser headed for the channel. When she came close aboard the crippled *Nevada*, Captain Scanland discovered a large gathering of his former crew assembled on the battered and grimy forecastle, a "spud's throw" away. Although the word, *Astoria,* had been removed from the stern of the cruiser, the battleship men knew that their former captain was on the bridge. They gave three rousing cheers for the "Old Man" and waved their white hats above their heads. They were glad that the skipper had been honored by this chance to engage the enemy. It must have been pathetic to see those splendid bluejackets, clothed in oily dungarees affectionately wishing God-speed to their popular captain. Father Walter has told me that he later ran across one of his *Astoria* shipmates, a Marine, in San Diego. The young corporal said, "I was an orderly on the bridge that day. The Old Man had tears in his eyes."

The *Astoria's* navigator, Lieutenant Commander William Guy Eaton, and his wife Edna, came to the Pacific Club one day with Father Mahler and Commander Charles Rend. We motored to the Oahu Country Club for lunch. At a table on the wide lanai which gave a view of the rolling fairways and the ocean beyond, we had a happy time, and Charlie Rend told a story. It was about the late Admiral James Raby whom I had known many years before. The Admiral was the uncle of Dan Calaghan and through him I got to know the Raby family. I saw the Admiral frequently when he was in command of the aircraft squadrons of the scouting force in the late twenties. He was known as an ardent Catholic, faithful always to his religious duties. Rend said that in the terrible Atlantic hurricane of 1917 when the Admiral, then a captain, was in command of the old cruiser *Albany,* he stood on the bridge, wondering, perhaps, whether the ship would capsize in the big blow. When the storm was at its height and great green waves hurtled over the bridge, someone telephoned from the engine room, "Sir, the chief machinist mate on the throttle is going crazy. He's reading the Bible out loud."

The officer of the deck passed the word to the Captain and the latter replied, "Tell them below the chief isn't so crazy. Tell them that the skipper is on the bridge saying his Rosary."

Bill Eaton had all the characteristics of the typical line officer of the Annapolis Navy. He was an exemplary husband and father. As an officer, he was endowed with a high sense of duty and he was delightfully human. Father Mahler once told me that each evening when the ship was at sea, after Eaton had "shot" the early stars, he came to the padre's room but always preceded by a mess boy who carried two glasses of Coca-Cola. Then a quiet chat about "Cabbages and Kings." The padre, knowing that Bill possessed a heavy leaning toward ice cream, used to "retaliate" with an occasional gift of the frozen delicacy which the mess boy delivered to the navigator's desk on the bridge.

I felt the pain of personal loss when word came that the gentle, soft-spoken Bill Eaton was killed at his post when the *Astoria* was lost in battle in the Solomons.

CHAPTER VIII

The Commission Pennant

ONE OF THE MOST pleasant features of my last cruise of four years in the Pacific Fleet was the chance it gave me to be with my friend Commander Charles J. Rend. Our friendship began at Brest, France, in 1918 where, as base chaplain, I met him after Mass one Sunday on board the destroyer tender, *Prometheus*. As an ardent Catholic, his unfailing attendance at Mass on my ship usually resulted, over the years, in our going ashore together Sunday afternoons in whatever section of the globe Navy ships were anchored.

Rend joined the Pacific Fleet at Pearl Harbor in the spring of 1941 and assumed command of a destroyer, a squadron leader. On Sundays, when his ship was at Pearl Harbor, he came to the *California*, not alone, but with a boatload of Catholic sailors of his command and led them to the forecastle where Mass was to be offered beneath the deck awning. It was truly inspiring to see him approach in the van of his faithful men and smile as he brought up a snappy Navy salute and exclaim, "Good morning, Padre. I've brought a few of the boys with me." His jovial, ruddy face and beaming eyes were a sight to cheer the heart. When I knew his ship was in port, it meant that Charlie would be over for Mass and Holy

Communion and that I should tell the mess boy to serve two late breakfasts in the wardroom.

After the Jap raid, Rend's ship had an enviable assignment. It belonged to the famous task force which Admiral William F. Halsey, Jr. commanded. The flagship was the doughty carrier, *Enterprise*. The formation called for the destroyer to steam out "in front," as it were, and spearhead the daring attacks on the Marshall Islands and later on Wake in the spring of 1942. When the story could be told, Charlie gave a vivid account of that thrilling raid.

The beginning of this story I got from Father John F. Hugues, the chaplain of the *Enterprise*. The day before the task force put to sea, Rend took his church party to the carrier for Mass. Delayed by last-minute preparations for rigging for a battle task, they arrived too late for the second Mass, but Father John offered a special third Mass for the skipper and his crew. All hands received Holy Communion. After Mass, they hurried to their destroyer, got under way, and headed for enemy country far to the southwest.

According to a former *California* shipmate, seaman Jim Walsh, who had been transferred to the destroyer, Commander Rend usually assembled the crew on the fantail of the destroyer leader shortly after getting underway and went over the operation orders and discussed the nature of the mission upon which they were embarked. It was the skipper's belief that the men were better fighting men when they knew the whole story and the exact part they were to play. The crew liked this frank discussion of things to come and they showed a lively interest and asked many intelligent questions.

The night before the attack on the Japanese bases in the Marshalls, the skipper sent for the first-class signalman, a young Polish-American lad by the name of Lloyd Vacovsky. "Ski," he said, "tomorrow at dawn we shall meet the enemy and we'll need God's help." In his hand, Commander Rend held a St. Christopher medal. He continued, "Break out a new commission pennant during the morning watch and sew this medal in the corner."

"Aye, aye, Sir," replied the lad as he left the bridge and promptly got busy.

The story of the raid was a thriller. The little destroyer contributed materially to the destruction of important installations on the Jap airfield. At one time they counted eighteen enemy planes overhead. It kept the skipper on the *qui vive* dodging the sticks of bombs as they fell from high altitudes.

On his return, Jim Walsh came to my office and praised his captain for his ability to be the first to spot the falling bombs. "He's a great skipper. I don't know how he does it. He knows just when to order 'hard right' or 'hard left' when we're makin' plenty knots and he sure gets us out of the way."

After the battle, the quartermaster lowered the long, sleek pennant, begrimed now by gases from the smoke-pipes, and handed it to his captain. St. Christopher had saved them from harm.

A few days after the return of the task force, the skipper invited Commander William W. Callaghan, brother of the late Rear Admiral, and me, to lunch with him on board the destroyer. Bill had recently arrived by clipper plane from the mainland. He was to take off in a few hours for San Francisco. After lunch, Rend had a mess boy get the pennant from his cabin. He spread it gently on the wardroom table. I felt reverently with my fingers the medal which "Ski" had sewed in the corner.

Commander Rend said, "Bill, I'd like you to take this pennant with you to San Rafael and give it to my boy Charlie." Then he rolled the narrow pennant thoughtfully and told the mess boy to make a neat package of it.

Months later, when I was ordered to San Francisco to preach at the cathedral on the anniversary of the Pearl Harbor raid, I paid a visit to the Rend home in San Rafael. There I saw the pennant hanging on the wall of little Charlie's room. The little fellow's mother and two sisters stood with me as we admired it. When little Charlie grows a bit older, he will treasure that bit of bunting as a symbol of a naval officer's faith in God, whom he loved and served with all his stout heart and heroic soul.

CHAPTER IX

Bread on the Waters

AMONG THE MORE trying tasks that daily faced me in my office was handling the requests of Navy wives to help them and their children to obtain berths on board the few ships that were available to evacuate families of service personnel to the mainland. It became necessary, in compliance with a despatch from Washington, to make up lists of those who lived in the Hawaiian Naval District and to embark them without show of partiality. At the top of each list were placed the names of the sick, but alas, it was impossible to please everyone. The telephone rang continuously and, between calls, women came with their children to the office and stressed their reasons for claiming the right to be the first to leave. At one time in December, there were over three thousand standing by to take passage for home. It did no good to explain that I had little or no connection with the business of evacuation, for they were quick to remind me that my recommendations would not go unheeded. They referred to a statement of policy which they had read in the papers to the effect that medical officers and chaplains would be consulted regarding the merits of doubtful cases.

I found it quite easy, however, to be patient with the individual problems of our Navy wives. For a quarter of a century in peace time, I had found countless reasons for sympathizing with Navy families on account of their nomadic way of living. The greater part of a Navy man's life is spent at sea, and this may account, strange as it may seem, for the fine family spirit he has of affection and loyalty. The Navy wife, unlike the Army wife who lives on a Government reservation, always faces, when she arrives at the port at which her husband's ship is based, the strenuous business of house hunting. Among my most vivid memories are the strange shacks and boarding houses Navy people called home years ago on the Asiatic Station. But they were cheerful about it and they still laugh when telling of their experiences. They will tell you about the many times they went "broke." Even though the Navy furnishes funds for transportation and the shipment of household effects, change of duty usually means spending the family's savings. Moving from the tropics to northern zones requires buying a new outfit of clothing for the family. Furniture, on arrival, is usually in need of repair; and the rents seem to grow unusually high when the Navy comes to town.

Departures of ships from Honolulu were made in military secrecy. Announcements of sailings came by telephone to the homes with only a few hours allotted for getting trunks and hand-bags to the dock. This uncertainty and the necessity of staying at all times near the family 'phone put ordinary shopping tours in the class of strategic planning. If someone failed to get the word about a sailing, there was always a willing substitute waiting with bag and baggage at the ship's gangway. Navy families for months literally lived "out of a suitcase."

As was to be expected, in accordance with ancient tradition, word got around that the chaplain could "fix it." There were hundreds who desired to remain in Honolulu.

When they found their names listed among those to go, not knowing that it would be unwise to load a ship entirely with sick people, they protested and suddenly thought, "maybe the chaplain can fix that too." Those without children who had jobs in the Navy Yard and in the city shops could not understand why they had to leave. Others, whose husbands were on duty on repair ships anchored in Pearl Harbor, felt they were being badly handled. The families of those who served in our cruisers and other ships which came in periodically for brief overhaul periods, wanted to remain because it would afford an occasional family reunion which they could not have had on the mainland. It was a difficult situation, and it was my job to be a sort of buffer between the wives and the Navy Yard officers whose unpleasant responsibility it was to make the final decisions.

The work of assisting the evacuées required one or more trips to the Navy Yard to plead my cases. An office had been established in the administration building, which was called the "Overseas Transport Service." The one in charge was an experienced officer of the regular Navy, Commander John B. Barrett. We had served together in 1930 in the Asiatic Fleet. I marvelled at the patience of this harried officer and I have since wondered how he kept going.

On entering his office, there was usually a crowd of women and children waiting for a chance to get the ear of one of Barrett's assistants or even the ear of Barrett himself. His job was anything but a sinecure. I actually felt sorry for him every time I came and presented, with a tear in my voice, the demands of some unhappy Navy wife who complained that the blackout was ruinous to her little boy's peace of mind, or the woman of wealth who had a palace in Pasadena which needed her personal supervision. Commander Barrett was so kind and sympathetic in squeezing so many of my clients on board the transports that I became eloquently profuse in my thanks.

He was particularly kind in helping me find a place on board a transport for Captain Barry Wilson's colored maid, Claribel. Barry and his wife Anne had brought the faithful Claribel with them when my old shipmate was ordered to Pearl Harbor following a cruise in the *Mississippi*. At the end of Barry's tour of duty there, Claribel decided to marry and live in Honolulu. But the war changed everything. She came to my office with her husband one day and asked me, "for old time's sake," to obtain passage for her and her little boy to the mainland. Commander Barrett did not spare himself on that assignment.

One day he laid down his pipe and, with a smile on his freckled face, exclaimed, "How can I refuse you? Don't you remember the night in Chefoo when my wife arrived alone from Tientsin? They told her there wasn't a room in town, not even a park bench. A ricksha coolie got hold of you and you scouted around until you found a room in Wineglass' boarding house. I wish I could forget, but I can't. All I can say is, 'Take it easy, chum; you're running me ragged.'" The Chefoo incident had vanished from my memory. Unknowingly, ten years before, I had cast Chinese bread upon the waters.

John Barrett was equal to the challenge of that heartbreaking emergency. I can still see him nervously pulling on his Dunhill pipe, checking the long list of evacuées and shaking his weary head to the accompaniment of a woeful, pidgin English, "No can do." But he salvaged his sense of humor, always finding time for a friendly chat. I seldom left his noisy office without a new story.

The Barretts' son was a remarkably bright child. His father often told me of his cleverness. One afternoon, with Father Mahler in tow, I drove out to his home on the Ala Wai to pay my respects. I had not seen Mrs. Barrett since that night of house hunting in Chefoo. John was about five years old, and a bright youngster. He showed us his menagerie of stuffed animals. It was the best variety of wild beasts I had ever seen. It struck me that Commander Barrett's old shipmates had the boy's collection in mind whenever they went ashore in strange and foreign ports of the world.

John had a little pigeon that came every morning for crumbs and sat outside the window while they both enjoyed the radio program. He flew away when John took the Army bus for school but he always returned when the child got back, for it was then time to play together on the front lawn.

John told us that he became worried one day when he heard that the Army was on the lookout for pigeons for the Signal Corps. He felt for a time that it was his duty in the war effort to suggest to his feathered buddy that he enlist. He figured the jig was up anyway; the Army's long arm would eventually reach out and get his pal.

When the Army's search for pigeons was well under way, John's pet disappeared. The little fellow knew then that the bird had been drafted. His disappointment was keen but he was grimly patriotic about it. For days, he pictured the pigeon in training as an Army private, learning to carry important messages that would thwart the enemy in his schemes.

After the neighbors had quit talking about Army pigeons and when John had almost forgotten the incident, one morning he discovered his bird-buddy again standing outside the window-screen, chipper and as good as new. At first John was elated but he could not quite make up his mind whether his pigeon had deserted the Army or whether his long absence simply proved that he had been too smart for the draft board.

When orders came for Father Mahler and me to proceed to San Diego for a tour of shore duty, Commander Barrett again showed that he meant what he said about the little favor I had done him in China. He visited at least three ships before deciding that he had found the one that would suit us. He had little to choose from and he was not a bit pleased with the results. He took us one day in June to a transport, a ship that for years had made the round-trip from New York to Havana, heavily laden with freight cars. It was really an old ferry-boat but it was the best thing afloat at the disposal of Commander John B. Barrett, U.S.N.

CHAPTER X

Kaneohe

AT KANEOHE BAY, on the windward side of the island of Oahu, the Navy built an air station the year before the outbreak of war and assigned Commander Harold M. Martin as the first commanding officer. When Martin, as a midshipman, starred at football at the Naval Academy, his classmates dubbed him "Beauty." But it was just for fun, for I believe they had in mind his brilliant game as a halfback rather than his militantly unbeautiful face. We had been shipmates for over two years on Vice Admiral Adolphus Andrews' staff when my chair was opposite his at the wardroom table of the flagship *Indianapolis*. Martin was the force aviator and when he was not in the air flying the Admiral's official plane, the smart "Blue Goose," he kept me busy supplying him with the latest important books in the ship's library. He was a good scholar.

We first met in April, 1938, in a domestic sort of way, at breakfast my first morning on board the heavy cruiser which was anchored off Long Beach, California. I overheard the soft voice of the rugged aviator announcing that his wife Beth was on the quest for a cook. As a former householder, I detected a "break" for Esme Gums, the colored maid at my hilltop home, Casa de Anita. My orders to sea and the departure of my little niece, Anita "Baba"

Nolan to the Flintridge Sacred Heart Academy, had placed our capable maid in the company of the unemployed. When I told "Beauty" the news of Esme's enforced idleness, he promptly had the staff motor-boat called alongside, sped to the Long Beach landing, and telephoned his wife. Without a moment's delay, Mrs. Martin motored posthaste to my late sister's home in Coronado, where Esme was temporarily housed, and signed up the West Indian cook for a tour of duty in the aviator's home. The Martins, especially their nine-year-old son David, liked Esme. She was happy too and not solely for the reason that among her chores was a weekly attendance at the movies with David in blissful tow.

Commander Martin and I were detached from Admiral Andrews' staff in the fall of 1940. The Bureau "fleeted me up" to the position of fleet chaplain as the relief of Captain Frank Harry Lash. My new home was the flagship *California*. On the bulkhead outside the door of my room hung a brass plate with the legend, "Fleet Chaplain." It shone like a Philadelphia doorknob and I little dreamed when it first dazzled my eyes that it would stand one day over the door of the living room of Casa de Anita, blackened with the oily waters of Pearl Harbor. The day the ship was raised from the muddy bottom in the spring of 1942, some unknown friend wrenched it from the bulkhead and gave it to me as a souvenir of December seventh.

The *California*, soon after I reported, led a "play wave" excursion of several ships to the mainland in order to give the officers and men a few days of leave in their homes. On my return to Pearl Harbor to take up my new duties as liaison officer ashore, I telephoned Commander Martin congratulations on his new assignment. Before giving me a chance to offer my services to his ship's company and their families, Beauty said, "How about coming over here next Sunday and holding Divine Services and Mass for my men?"

It is one of the consoling rewards of long service in the Navy to find a former shipmate, whom you knew as a cog-in-the-wheel, in a position of great responsibility. As a young chaplain, I wondered if I should ever be able to call the "Old Man" by his nickname. A commanding officer is necessarily a recluse on board ship, lest familiarity be given a chance to breed contempt. The captain lives severely alone and takes his meals alone in his cabin. He may not "mix" with his officers. He is like a bishop in that respect and he commands a sort of reverence by virtue of the vital position he holds. Growing old in the service has had its compensations. I finally reached the point where Tom, Dick and Harry of the old wardroom days eventually rose to the command of ships. When I went aboard to see them on duty or to dine, they were happily still Tom, Dick and Harry to me. I got a boyish thrill from calling the big boss of the Kaneohe air station, "Beauty."

His prompt concern about the spiritual welfare of his outfit did not surprise me, for Martin had attended faithfully whenever I held general services on board the *Indianapolis* at sea.

The next Sunday, in the cool of early morning, I motored over the Pali and down the windward side of the verdant mountain and on across the plain to Kaneohe Bay. The station was about twenty miles from Honolulu though it never seemed that far. I never tired of the round-trip. It was the most delightful motor ride I have ever enjoyed anywhere in the world. The emerald green of the wooded cliffs and the lighter green of the plantation fields below prepared one's enchanted eye for the fascinating jade tints of the sea beyond. It is a wonder I ever arrived on time.

Commander Martin had made careful preparations. The services, which were the first ever conducted on the station, were held in the new auditorium. Officers and their ladies and hundreds of bluejackets attended. An officer's wife played the piano for the congregational singing and another talented wife sang a solo. At the close of the general service, I heard confessions and offered Holy Mass for the Catholic men. As a reward for my labors, the hospitable Martins took me to their quarters for breakfast. This became, for several months, the Sunday morning routine whenever the *California* was at sea. When the ship was in port, I motored to Pearl Harbor and offered Mass on the forecastle.

One day after the December raid, I sat with Commander Martin in his office. In true Navy style, he ordered coffee to be served. In the course of our conversation, he told me what had happened to him when the Japs attacked the station. He said that he and his son David were in the living room of their quarters. The Commander, clad in pajamas, was toying with a cup of coffee. They both heard planes overhead coming in, as they thought, for a landing. Martin, when he got a view of them, exclaimed, "Great balls of tar—they're coming in the wrong way; they're violating the rules. . . ."

Young David, with the quick eye of a boy enthusiast, grabbed his father by the arm and shouted, "Hey, daddy, they're Japs. . . . see the Rising Sun on the fuselage."

The Commander, like a city fireman, jumped into his uniform and sprinted to his office. Jap Zeros were "strafing" the planes and hangars.

Many tales were told of the heroism of Martin's officers and men and it was gratifying to hear everyone speak with especial pride of the fearlessness and charity of Mrs. Martin and her group, made up of the wives of officers and enlisted men. They worked all day and night to the point of exhaustion, caring for the wounded, and they proved that women too can face the enemy without fear.

At the Naval Training Station in San Diego one afternoon in the spring of 1943, a stalwart, blue-eyed aviation radioman called on me. He was Romeo E. Guilbert, a boy from Somerville, New Jersey, whom I had met at Kaneohe Bay. He came over from North Island to have a chat about old times and he reminisced about the Jap raid, telling how the Zeros strafed for twenty minutes, firing incendiaries and explosive shells.

Guilbert said he was standing in front of a hangar when the Japs dived over the station. The many big bombers at anchor in the bay and others parked on the ramp they destroyed with explosive shells. Guilbert modestly omitted telling of his own heroic work during the raid, and spoke only of his shipmates. He gave a vivid account of two brothers who ran out together under the Jap bullets, climbed into a PBY plane and turned a machine gun on the enemy planes. Many of his shipmates were killed. Guilbert continued, "It's strange how things strike you as funny at a time like that. Take my friend Simmons, for example. A Zero, which can be maneuvered like a scooter, made a pass at him and instead of seeking cover, Simmons ran around the corner of the laundry with the Zero chasing him. That Jap must have had a sense of humor. He kept chasing Simmons for two laps around that laundry and never even scratched him. We sure kidded Simmons when the show was over."

Another story was not so pleasant but it revealed something fine in Guilbert's character. He told of seeing a shipmate killed at his gun. The young sailor had occupied a bunk next to Guilbert in the barracks. My friend said, "He was the most jolly fellow I ever knew, always laughing about something, and he kept us all in good humor. The morning after the raid when I awoke, I looked over toward his bunk expecting to see his smiling face—but he wasn't there. It stunned me. Gosh, how we missed that guy!"

Guilbert's squadron of Catalinas took off that evening bound for Kaneohe Bay.

From the air station, when promoted to the rank of captain, Harold Martin was ordered to assume command of Midway. His influence will long be felt at Kaneohe as was attested one day in April, 1943, when Rear Admiral David W. Bagley, Commandant of the 11th Naval District, visited the training station at San Diego. With our commanding officer, Captain Henry C. Gearing, the Admiral, who had lately been District Commandant of the Hawaiian Area, inspected our new North Chapel. As these officers left the chapel to continue their tour of inspection, Admiral Bagley turned to me and said, "You have a lovely chapel and I am sure the men are proud of it. Just before leaving Pearl Harbor a few weeks ago, 'Gotch' Dillon, the commanding officer of the air station at Kaneohe Bay, came to me and said, 'There are two things we need at Kaneohe—a swimming pool and a chapel.'"

From the expression on the Admiral's face, I felt that my old shipmate, Captain Wallace M. Dillon, who relieved Beauty Martin got what he wanted.

Near a sand dune, about a mile from the air station, there is a new cemetery where eighteen officers and men lie in the shade of friendly palm trees. A few paces from the row of crosses stands a solitary wooden marker painted with the words, "Lieutenant ————— Aviator, Imperial Navy of Japan." An American sailor had avenged his Kaneohe shipmates.

CHAPTER XI

The Finger Print

THE UNITED STATES MARINE, our soldier of the sea, has well merited his reputation as the world's toughest fighter. His performance at Wake and Guadalcanal showed him true to his corps' motto, *"Semper Fidelis."* But you will also find him revealing a high sense of duty while standing an unexciting watch at the Navy Yard gate. It was only natural to expect that the orders to the Pearl Harbor Marines, immediately following the Japanese raid, would make them particularly exacting when examining passes of those seeking entrance into the Pearl Harbor Navy Yard. Although we were never out of uniform, the Marine sentries studiously examined our identification cards which carried our thumb prints and the little rogues' gallery portraits. When the sentry finally deigned to let us enter through the solemn portals, it made us feel almost guilty of some forgotten breach of the regulations. The photograph on my pass which had been made by the *Nevada's* ship's photographer during the passage to Hawaii in the spring of 1941, showed me in a blue blouse. It occurred to me that a picture in khaki might make it easier for the gate sentry inasmuch as we never wore blues in Hawaii, and I wore whites only on formal occasions.

One morning, while walking through the repair basin

of the yard on my way to the photo shop of the receiving station, I ran across a sailor who had stopped on the pier near a destroyer which I recognized as the old *Litchfield* in which, in 1923, I had made a cruise in the Black Sea. In those days, I had a roving commission in the destroyer squadron that based at Constantinople and I made many interesting cruises in several destroyers visiting all the important towns on the Black Sea and the shores of the Eastern Mediterranean. My purpose in moving from one ship to another was to get acquainted with the men of the squadron.

I recognized the bluejacket immediately and he remembered me. Sensing my uneasiness at not being able to recall his name, he said he was Jim Warren and that he served in those days as a seaman second class in the fo'csle division. As we stood there reminiscing on those happier days in the Middle East and the tragic morning of December seventh, I asked him if he recalled that the *Litchfield* was named for a bluejacket who was killed in France while serving with the Marines as a pharmacist's mate. He said he did and he thought that fact might have had something to do with the extraordinary pride the men took in the *Litchfield*. I told him of the day I had lunch in the wardroom when the ship was at anchor in the Bosporus near the Sultan's palace. Sitting opposite me was the late Dr. George White, one of the squadron medicos. Having taken a rather active part in the general conversation, the Doctor suddenly lost interest in what we others were saying and stared at a brass plaque which hung on the bulkhead just over my right shoulder. He looked sad and I inquired what was troubling him. With a slight hint of a tear in his eye, he replied, "As many times as I have been on board this ship, I never suspected that she was named for my corpsman, Litchfield. He was with me in Belleau Wood. Under fire one morning, he volunteered to go out into 'no-man's land' and rescue a wounded Marine who lay in a shell crater. On his way back with the man slung over his shoulder, Litchfield was killed by shrapnel. So they named this destroyer for him. I should have known; he was a brave kid."

Jim Warren remembered the beach picnic I organized one day for the *Litchfield* men at Samsun when most of us got so sun-burned that we were for days virtually useless. We also talked about the Armenian refugees and what a hard time they had under the heel of the ruthless Turk. We parted at Merry Point Landing where the sailor boarded a motor launch for one of the carriers. It may have been the chance meeting with the *Litchfield* shipmate or maybe it was the thumb print I made that morning on the identification card that caused me to recall an incident which took place the week the *Litchfield* spent at Samsun.

The day before the destroyer dropped anchor off the little Turkish village on the south shore of the Black Sea, three thousand Armenians limped down the dusty road to town and, finding no shelter, spread their blankets in the open fields. They were victims of "deportation." The Turks had driven them from their homes beyond the mountain range of Anatolia. Those who survived the rigors of the long and bloody trek, hoped to be taken by steamer to Greece and given a chance to start life over again.

One day, an agent of the Near East Relief Society, named Hart, invited me to accompany him on a tour of inspection of the many refugee compounds. The next morning, I took the *Litchfield's* motor dory and found Hart waiting for me on the jetty. As we walked down the narrow street, I caught a glimpse of the hills which gave the town a crescent frame of faint purple, that faded steadily to a rich green as the eye traced its descent to the rocky road and the mosque where the town begins. The thought came to me: Nature at its loveliest and man at his worst. We passed open shops on the sidewalk; food lay in a blazing sun exposed to a million flies; bedraggled Armenian women and children, half-naked and nearly starved, darted nervously among surly Turks, snatching a morsel of food from the shelves and escaping like frightened rabbits.

We came to a large church. It was no longer used as a place of worship. Refugees lived there; women and little children slept on the floor and the men found refuge in the cellar. Those who were ill were permitted by the agent to lie on the floor of the cool interior but the rest were made to do chores, unless their old age entitled them to bask in the morning sun. Over in a far corner of the building stood an old priest of the Greek Orthodox Church. He had accompanied his flock on the long march and won from Hart a job as overseer of the place. He had the aura of an Old Testament Patriarch, with his long beard, shaggy eyebrows and deep-set piercing eyes. He wore a biretta that looked like a candy box and his cassock was in tatters. There was tragedy in his look but no sign of despair, as he approached and bowed. Hart's interpreter, a Moslem named Mahmud, came up to us and gave, in broken English, the priest's report of the morning.

"There is no news of the stolen money," said Mahmud, "but the woman suspect will be at Mr. Hart's office at ten o'clock." Hart explained to me that someone had robbed an Armenian woman of the equivalent of seventy dollars with which she hoped to buy a passage to Piraeus. The suspect had slept alongside the victim the night the money disappeared. "Let's go," said Hart. "I've got an idea."

Hart escorted me through several compounds where Armenians lived in close congestion. We sampled soup from steaming pots in the yard. We inspected the rooms of the barracks and studied the faces of the younger men as Mahmud translated the admonitions of Hart when he found conditions unsanitary. This relief worker performed many of the functions of a shepherd. If your imagination allowed you to overlook the quality of the tweed of his golf suit and to fancy a crook in his hand instead of a malacca cane, he looked like one.

Each house we visited had a Greek Orthodox priest in charge. They too were shepherds. Mahmud, the Turk, was indispensable. Many questions were asked regarding the sailings to Constantinople. Quarrels had to be settled, for men will argue when their nerves are on edge.

We hurried down a narrow street; it was nearly ten o'clock. We arrived at a frame building and climbed the stairs to the second floor. From one of the windows of the office, I saw a veiled Turkish woman hanging clothes on a line. The other window behind Hart's desk gave out on a field where the Armenians squatted in family circles. There were priests moving among them. I saw one in a ragged cassock strolling from one group to another, patting the children's heads and listening to the woeful tales of their parents.

The door suddenly opened. Two Turkish soldiers dragged a woman into the room and placed her before Hart's desk. Mahmud followed them. The woman was dressed in a gunny sack; her feet were bare and her matted hair fell in uneven strands over her bony shoulders. She was terror-stricken.

"Mahmud." Hart's voice was loud and sharp. "Tell this woman that unless the money is returned within three days, I'll give no more food to the refugees. She knows who took it. Tell her that."

Mahmud delivered the ultimatum. The Turks carried the screeching woman through the doorway. I could hear her protesting all the way down the stairs.

"Do you think that'll work?" I asked Hart. "Anyone mean enough to steal seventy dollars from a refugee won't worry about your stopping the food supply."

"You'll see," was Hart's answer. He was obviously worried.

A few days later, Hart came off to the ship for lunch. I inquired about his detective work and he said his plan had failed. The three days of grace had passed and Hart had to make good his threat. He was a kind-hearted fellow and the idea of stopping the rations disturbed him. For advice, he went to the old priest who was in charge of the big church. The priest said, "I will find the thief. Get me two sticks of wood and a bucket of paint. Call my people to the church. I will catch the thief."

After the mid-day meal, the refugees crowded into the church, where they found their pastor standing beyond the sanctuary rail, holding high a crudely made cross. On the rail near him stood a pail of white paint. With a loud, bass voice, the old patriarch ordered his people to come up the center aisle and to dip the index finger into the paint and then to touch the cross. Before they started to move toward the rail, the priest explained the strange ritual, and he stressed the sacred importance of their testimony. Mahmud stood near Hart and translated the sermon. In spite of the crowd of men, women and children, it was silent in the church. The refugees slowly moved up the aisle with their sad eyes fixed upon the cross.

When half had testified with their finger print of paint, a young man came up. He held his hands behind him. When he stood before the priest, he whispered something. The priest lowered the cross and ordered the others to leave. He took the young man by the arm and led him to the sacristy. In a moment he returned with a roll of paper money in his hand and solemnly gave it to the relief worker.

Hart was impressed by the successful tactics of the priest. He understood that the old pastor had made an appeal to the thing the young man held most sacred—his Faith. In spite of the assurance of escape to Greece which the stolen money would have guaranteed, the repentant thief proved he was a true Christian when put to the Holy test.

CHAPTER XII

Commander Scouting Force

DRIVING ONE MORNING through the Pearl Harbor Navy Yard, I discovered that one of my old sea-homes had just arrived from the battle area. In her war disguise of mud-colored paint, she no longer resembled the well-groomed thoroughbred. War had changed her complexion but she now looked tougher and I felt proud that I was not a stranger on her decks.

I went to the quarterdeck and asked if the chaplain, my old friend, Razzie W. Truitt, were on board, and as I turned to go forward to his room, saw my Methodist colleague heading my way. He was the proud veteran of many a sea fight, looking a bit tired but as usual he was bursting with good humor. Although we did not know it then, Truitt was later to get orders to relieve me as fleet chaplain. That morning, after we paid a call on the skipper, Captain Edward W. Hanson, we crossed the dry-dock to the *San Francisco* and called on my friend, Captain Daniel J. Callaghan, who, that fall, as a rear admiral, gave his life in the battle off Savo Island in the Solomons. We had coffee with the former presidential aide in his cabin. He looked worn out but he said he hoped to get in a few sets of tennis that afternoon.

We left the *San Francisco*, and again went to my old ship. It was my last time on board the cruiser. That evening, sitting in the blackout of my lanai at the Pacific Club, I thought of the two and one-half years I had spent in that happy ship.

The president of the wardroom mess was Commander Ralph O. Davis and he sat at the head of the senior table by virtue of his job as executive officer of the ship. The popular "exec" was greatly responsible for the home-like atmosphere of the wardroom. Although the rank of the members ranged from ensign to captain, there was no "springing" of rank on the "J. O's." Our wardroom seemed more like the living room of a happy home. The most popular game was dominoes but the mess boasted several good bridge players and kibitzers, too. The "exec" usually promoted and organized wardroom dinner parties on board or ashore. This gave us a chance to know the families of our mess mates, for there was hardly time, what with the strenuous operation schedule of the fleet, to make a social circuit of the homes.

I liked particularly the dinner parties we held on board. One Christmas day a few years ago, after Mass, the boats came off to the ship loaded to the gunwales with wives and children of officers and men. They all stayed aboard for dinner. Children of the enlisted men dined in the gaily decorated mess hall of the sailors, and the officers' families had dinner in the wardroom. Rear Admiral John F. Shafroth, who was then a captain and commanded the ship, was the guest of honor. I had promised my sister Anita to have Christmas dinner with her family in Coronado; and as I hurried through the crowded wardroom to catch a boat, the mess boys were about to serve dinner. Ralph Davis called to me, "Hello, Padre—Merry Christmas. Won't you say grace for us?" It was a thoughtful tribute to my position as chaplain.

Ralph and I were shore-going pals whenever the ship separated him from his wife Dorothy and their son "Skip" who by this time must boast a commission in the armed forces. One day which I fondly remember we motored from Long Beach to my home in the hills. While Skip rode horseback with my sister's children, Ralph and I demonstrated without effort how two seafaring men can appreciate the country. In March, 1943, I heard Ralph's voice on the telephone. He called late in the evening and said he had just arrived from the Solomons where the Japs had sunk the cruiser *Chicago* which he commanded. Ralph, of course, was the last one to leave the doomed ship. He was now heading East to take command of a new ship.

The other officers at our table were members of Admiral Andrews' staff. They were experts in their specialties and I felt that they, when added up, were an animated encyclopedia. "Pay" Rose, the force paymaster, was expected to have all the answers when Commander Robert O. "Chick" Glover, the force engineer, slyly posed a problem of national finance. Between Commander Davis and me sat the force medical officer, Captain Alfred J. Toulon. Our names again appeared on the same roster of officers when I was assigned to the training station at San Diego.

One evening at sea, Admiral Andrews invited Dr. Toulon and me to dine with him in his cabin. Knowing his reputation as a raconteur, I was hopeful the Force Commander might tell us a few of his favorite yarns. His naval career had exemplified how versatile he was. There have not been many officers in the history of the Navy who have succeeded so well in so many exacting assignments. As a seagoing officer, he had held many important commands; one was the battleship *Texas*. When I served in the *Mississippi* in 1934, Admiral Andrews was chief of staff of the United States Fleet and aide to my former skipper, Admiral Joseph M. Reeves, the Commander in Chief. Before taking command of the scouting force, he had completed a tour of duty in Washington as chief of the Bureau of Navigation. This department is now called the Bureau of Naval Personnel. But I have always thought of Admiral Andrews as the distinguished naval aide of Presidents Harding and Coolidge.

That evening at table, he recalled an incident which took place when he was aide to Calvin Coolidge. The President and the Admiral, who was then a captain, stood in one of the halls of the White House talking generalities, when suddenly the President said, "Andrews, are you a Catholic?" His aide replied that he was not. The President continued, "Tomorrow we attend Mass at St. Matthew's Church. You'd better find out when to stand up and when to kneel down. Good night."

This had put it squarely up to the aide. For a moment, Captain Andrews was a bit nonplussed until he discovered the presence of an old Irish doorkeeper who for years had worked in the White House. The Captain spoke to him, "Pat, are you a Catholic?"

"Sure and I am, Sir," said Pat.

"Fine—do you know when to stand up and kneel down at Mass?"

"Of course, Sir. I used to serve the priest's Mass when I was a boy."

This was good news. "Very well, Pat. Tonight I'll get you a cutaway coat and a pair of striped trousers, for tomorrow at St. Matthew's you'll sit in front of the President of the United States. When you stand up, he'll stand up—and you'd better be right."

The Admiral could tell a good story mighty well.

I never went to the Admiral's cabin on official business unless I had studied every angle and had my decision made before offering it to him for approval. When you arrived, he was gracious to a fault. But when you had sat upon the comfortable leather chair at the corner of his desk and accepted a smoke, the Admiral closed his eyes to concentrate, and you had the floor. At times he opened his eyes and nodded, "Yes" or "No," and his face lighted up. At the end, when he made the decision, he was again cordial and he smiled as you, with a "Good morning, Sir," promptly made for the door that led to the passageway.

Admiral and Mrs. Andrews and their daughter Frances then lived in a fine house beyond Diamond Head. One afternoon I went to call and enjoyed a delightful hour on their lanai which gave a view of the opalescent sea. Our conversation swung to the years I had spent as a seminarian at Louvain, Belgium. I rather expected the Admiral would ask me whether I had met Cardinal Mercier. He finally did and it gave me a chance to say that I had heard that he had once served as the Cardinal's Naval Aide when the famous Belgium patriot visited the United States. The Admiral told me he had spent three weeks with the Cardinal and had gotten to know him intimately. "In my opinion," he said, "Cardinal Mercier was the greatest man who ever came to our country."

Here I interrupted, "May I quote you some day, Admiral?"

With a soft, mellow voice and eyes aglow, Admiral Andrews replied, "You certainly may, Padre—he was a great man—the greatest ever to come to our shores."

The Commander Scouting Force (as the boys say) "had everything." If the members of his staff and the officers and men of his flagship were noticeably above average in appearance and in performance of duty, it was because Vice Admiral Adolphus Andrews showed the way.

CHAPTER XIII

Tears in the Bucket

DURING THE WEEK at 7 A.M., I offered daily Mass at the Sacred Heart altar in the Cathedral of Our Lady of Peace, in Honolulu. To arrive in the cheerless blackout a little before seven and see Brother Paschal, the sacristan, arranging the vestments in the semi-darkness of the sacristy, was like a bracing tonic, for in spite of the tragic war news, his optimism never deserted him. He would say, "Good morning, Father—how's the war going?" Or, "Things look better today, don't they?" Paschal was a lay brother of the Missionary Order of the Sacred Hearts of Jesus and Mary. He was like a boatswain in a ship, having full charge of the "equipage" of the rather large cathedral. Among his chores was the organizing and training of a staff of acolytes for daily service at the altar. His crew was a cross-section of the many races that had come to the Islands and it was not easy for him, a Belgian, to keep them in line.

One morning after Mass, I complimented Brother Paschal on the smart performance of the little Korean boy who had given the Latin responses perfectly and had shown reverence and carefulness in every little task assigned him. He was so small, that I feared he would drop the large missal whenever the time came to carry it from one side of the altar to the other. I told the sacristan that

80

his was the best trained outfit of altar boys I had ever seen, not forgetting my old boyhood mates at St. Joseph's in Paterson, New Jersey.

"Well," said Brother Paschal, "I try to teach my boys the meaning of discipline. I romp with them at our summer camp and joke with them in the locker room and I praise them when they do well. But they shake in their boots when I crack down. They know I mean business when it comes to their work in the sanctuary." It was apparent that Brother Paschal had instilled in his altar boys a high sense of duty.

I grew fond of these missionaries who, for many years, have labored in the Hawaiian Islands. Like Father Damien, most of them had come from Belgium and chose to remain in Hawaii for the balance of their lives. I feel indeed lucky to have known quite well the late Bishop Stephen Alencastre, a member of the missionary order; he was universally loved in the Islands. He often invited me to lunch or dinner in his home and he impressed me deeply by his understanding and charity as a true shepherd of souls. He was in poor health when I last saw him and this made him appear doubly ascetic and frail. But he kept active to the end and died on board ship on his way to San Francisco where he had planned to attend an important meeting in the fall of 1940. Bishop Stephen, as he was fondly called by everyone, was the last of the missionary bishops. A year after his death, the Holy Father sent as the first Bishop of the Diocese of Honolulu, the Most Reverend James J. Sweeney, D.D., who will be known some day perhaps as the "War Bishop."

Among the missionaries of Hawaii, the man whom the men of the Navy know best is the famous Father Valentin. He is now in his eighties but his spirit is still as young as on the day he landed on the island of Oahu to be the successor of Father Damien of Molokai. For some good reason, Father Valentin was ordered instead to an important job in Honolulu which deprived him of the honor of serving among the lepers. His record on Oahu reveals what great things he might have done had he carried on in the footsteps of the saintly Damien.

I first met the tall and rugged Father Valentin over twenty years ago when the *Idaho* visited the Islands. For all intents and purposes, he then was and for many years continued to be, the Catholic chaplain of the Pearl Harbor Navy Yard.

During the week, he attended the sick at the Naval Hospital, often driving ten miles from town in the middle of the night to give the last rites to a dying sailor. On Sunday mornings, after offering a five o'clock Mass in the territorial prison, he motored to the old Y.M.C.A. hut in the Yard where he heard confessions, celebrated Mass and preached. His altar, which is still in use in the Navy Yard, Father Valentin built at his own workbench in the Mission House. After his second Mass, the grand old warrior took the ferry to Ford Island and celebrated a third Mass for the families and men of the air station. For over twenty years, this was Father Valentin's Sunday morning routine. It was, for a man of his years, an heroic achievement, and I was glad when Bishop Stephen ordered him to turn over his Navy Yard duties to Chaplain Father Thomas J. Odlum in the winter of 1941. Father Valentin's love for the Navy and his superb sense of duty in quest of souls, made no allowances for his age. He was indefatigable, and he used to startle me by the indifference he showed toward his crippled leg. But the doctor occasionally caught up with him and exiled the old priest to a hospital bed.

Navy people on their rounds of the globe see strange sights and meet unusual "characters," and they return "homeside" anxious to tell you about them. I believe there is no one more frequently mentioned or more dearly loved than Father Valentin of Pearl Harbor. When the Secretary of the Navy, the Hon. Frank Knox, learned that Father Valentin no longer was ministering to the men of the Navy, he wrote the beloved missionary a splendid letter; it read like a naval citation.

When I last saw my old friend, he was living in a little house on the grounds of St. Francis Hospital in Honolulu. With funds his friends had given him, he built a little place of retirement with the understanding that it would become the property of the Sisters when he died.

I believe I shall always remember Father Valentin for his extraordinary sense of duty. Along with a jolly sense of humor, perfect unselfishness and tolerance toward the errors and foibles of his fellow man, his steadfast will to keep on the job for the honor and glory of God should certainly secure him a place among the immortals.

A few days after the Jap raid, I went to the Pearl Harbor Hospital to visit the wounded. In one of the wards, I ran across a sailor from the *Arizona* who, in spite of his severe burns, seemed to want someone to talk to. It was mostly about the "blitz" that he talked and there is one incident of that awful morning that high-lighted the others that he mentioned. It had to do with that paramount attribute of the true service man—sense of duty.

The young sailor had been burned in the blast of a

bomb and started dizzily toward the quarterdeck. He said, "When I got there, I was scared and hurt and lost my head. I might have jumped over the side if I hadn't bumped into Lieutenant Commander Fuqua, the first lieutenant of the ship. He was walking about calmly, ordering men to seek cover and, with no thought of himself, he managed everything on the quarterdeck. Hell was breakin' loose but one look at him made me snap out of it. I got calm myself and I waited patiently for someone to help me over the side and into a boat."

Lieutenant Commander Samuel G. Fuqua was awarded the Navy Cross for his service that morning, "above and beyond the call of duty."

That same afternoon I stopped at the bed of Ensign Henry D. Davison who had been wounded while officer of the deck on board the *Arizona* during the raid on Pearl Harbor. I asked Davison whether he recalled any acts of extraordinary bravery that morning. At first, he simply said, "All hands performed magnificently. I couldn't have asked for better men." Later, with feeling, he told of ordering Harry Ray, a boatswain's mate second class, to telephone the central engine room and ask for more pressure on the fire main. While in the telephone booth, a bomb struck close by and the flames enveloped Ray. But he stayed in the booth, trying his best to get the message through. Davison said that he hurried to the booth to order Ray to a safer place when another blast got both of them. They were severely burned. Another bomb exploded near the booth and Davison jumped overboard and swam to a boat. He did not know then what became of the heroic Harry Ray, but it was evident that the boatswain's mate will always be one of Davison's heroes.

I once came face to face with sense of duty manifested by two little boys. One night from the deathbed of my sister Anita, a young mother of four children, I sped from San Diego, California, to the foothills to tell her children the tragic news. When I reached the gate of their country place, two of the boys, Jack, fourteen years old and Roger Michael, ten, who had lately learned to milk the family cow, jumped the rail fence of the corral and climbed onto the running board of the car. They feared the worst but said not a word. Over the years of my priestly life, I had had similar duties to perform but this was the most difficult task I had ever undertaken. When the car reached their home on the top of the knoll, I found my niece, Anita, and her little brother Bill standing in the darkness with the faithful colored maid Adelaide Gumbs. I was deeply affected. All the way from the hospital, I had repeatedly said to my friend Father Francis J. Burke, a fellow navy chaplain, "Frank, I've done this thing all my life but now I don't know how to begin." When the moment came, I gathered all four children around me but all I could say was, "Kids, your dear mother has gone to heaven." In the confusion and weeping that naturally followed, a kind neighbor took Anita and little Bill by the hand and walked across the lawn to console them. But the two amateur farm hands had disappeared in the darkness. When I asked Father Burke where they had gone, he replied, "They said they had a job to finish. I last saw them stumbling down the hill to the corral. God love 'em. There'll be many a tear in that bucket of milk tonight."

CHAPTER XIV

Flowers for the Lord

WHY NAVY MEN SEEM to acquire, especially at sea, an affectionate interest in the sacred drama of Mass, has often been the subject of comment among my fellow chaplains. It may be because so many, in the manner of scene-shifters in a theatre, have so much to do with "staging" the performance.

When the hour comes for rigging for church, the bluejackets and the chaplain start at scratch to erect the scenery and gather the properties for the Divine Service. The only article furnished by the ship's blueprint is the deck. Everything else the men lug from below. When the bosun's mate and his men get the word to "rig for church," a varied assortment of orders direct members of the working party to assemble first the altar which the men carry up a ladder from below deck and then carefully take off the canvas sack which had protected it for a week. Mess attendants know it is time to carry rugs from the wardroom and lay them carefully before the altar. The wardroom steward, if he has been ashore during the morning and bought flowers, arranges them in the altar vases. Behind the altar, another party of men rig the crimson velour curtain which serves handsomely as a dossal. Then come others carrying the ship's piano, mess benches and chairs while others secure the canvas windbreaks to keep the altar things from being blown over the side.

When the chaplain arrives with his Mass kit, there are usually volunteers to help him dress the altar. It is then that the chaplain realizes that the men have become intimately acquainted with something that formerly they had viewed only at a mystic distance. They ask questions about the altar stone, admitting they had never before seen one. They examine the chalice with curious eyes and seem glad to be allowed to come so close to the sanctum sanctorum. I have made it a practice at sea to vest at the altar and explain as I go along the history and meaning of each article from the amice to the chasuble. I believe the Navy man really participates at Mass with more understanding than his civilian brother.

I sometimes wonder whether my shipmates in the destroyer *McCormick* in the early twenties have ever told their landsmen friends of the Masses they attended on our cruises in the Black Sea and the eastern Mediterranean. Sundays, the ship rolled and pitched so much that my altar boys were required to assist me in strange rubrics which you will not find in our books on liturgy. On those difficult Sundays, one sailor held the altar in place; another got a grip on the missal stand; another the chalice and still another, braced against a stanchion, tried with his free arm to keep me on an even keel.

At the air station on Kaneohe Bay, Hawaii, I found that the sailors were not unlike my former shipmates in the fleet. Sitting on the auditorium chairs, they were not so close to the altar as the men who attended Mass on mess benches in the forward compartment of the destroyer *McCormick* or on the forecastle of the *California*. But soon after my first Mass there, they were quick to suggest that the station carpenter build an altar and a lectern, which they called a pulpit. Arriving one Sunday morning, I found a delegation of sailors proudly lugging a new altar to the center of the stage. Its white enamel glistened and the artistic gold cross on the frontal panel was a high achievement in naval carpentry. This was their tribute to the Divine Service.

On Palm Sunday in 1942 at the air station, an ensign came to me after Mass and said, "The men have asked me to find out if you would object to their taking up a collection for Easter flowers. They would like to chip in and make the altar look fine for Easter Mass."

With the money collected during Holy Week, a committee of sailors went to Honolulu and bought a truckload of flowers. On Easter morning, the altar and the improvised Sanctuary were resplendent with the varied hues of the glorious flowers of Oahu. Floral beauty expressed the sailor's way of celebrating the feast of our Savior's resurrection.

Motoring back to Honolulu that Easter day, I thought of flowers and how they give eloquence to our thoughts and feelings. On long cruises, a man-o-war's man secretly yearns for the trees and the bushes in the woods and the violets and roses that bloom near his home. An officer is grateful to the steward who brings flowers to the wardroom on the eve of a cruise. He knows that the steward has also carried aboard water from town because the distilled water made on board is not able to keep life in the flowers for long. He knows, too, that those flowers will appear on the altar on Sunday morning.

As I drove along the shoreline toward Koko Head, where I fancied I could see beyond the misty horizon the island of Molokai, I recalled a story a missionary priest had told me in Honolulu. He spoke of the time the body of Father Damien, the leper priest, lay in state before the high altar in the Cathedral of Our Lady of Peace. A boat was then at the pier which, in a few days, would carry the mortal remains of the saintly priest to his last resting place in Belgium. The missionary said that the physician, who many years ago had attended Father Damien in the leper colony just prior to his death, was now living in Honolulu. The doctor found a way of paying a loving tribute to his martyred friend. Each morning, the aged and feeble gentleman came to the cathedral carrying a bouquet of gardenias, and he laid it solemnly beside the casket. Perhaps he remembered that Father Damien, too, was a lover of flowers.

When I returned to my home in the foothills beyond San Diego, after spending four years at sea, it delighted me to convert a small plot of ground into a rose garden. Every day after office hours at the training station, I worked the soil and acquired a group of new friends "set free by summer's earliest duty." When they bloomed, it became a joy to place the roses on the altar of my private chapel.

Late one morning, many years ago, I visited the sacristy of St. Mark's in Venice. It was in August, the morning after Our Blessed Lady's feast-day. I cannot recall why I was there for I was a young student then but I shall always remember the old priest who was vesting in preparation for offering Holy Mass. He was a kindly, frail little man with silvery hair and so feeble that he seemed barely able to throw the heavily embroidered chasuble over his head. Near the place where he stood was a water font, carved in marble and embedded in the ancient wall of the sacristy. Above the opening where the water flowed, was a receptacle carved out of the same block of Carrara marble and in it stood a dewy, fresh calla lily. Before taking the chalice in his hands and walking across the long room to a side altar in the Basilica, the old priest went to the font, placed his wrinkled fingers under the flowing water and, having used the snow-white towel to dry them, gently touched the pure petals of the lily. This was his simple tribute to the sacred function he was soon to perform. The symbolism of this simple act of reverence made an indelible impression on my young mind.

During the days following the Pearl Harbor raid, there stood on the table of my room at the Pacific Club a picture of Our Savior showing symbolically His Sacred Heart. It was a little picture in a metallic frame which I had for years carried with me in Navy ships. As it stood on my table, flanked by papers and pencils, it did not occur to me that I had been neglectful until one evening I discovered two hibiscus blooms and ginger buds lying before it. I knew then that Nakayama San, the housemaid, had taught me a lesson. The old Japanese maid, each morning, brought fresh flowers and placed them before the picture of the Sacred Heart. When I thanked her, she bowed and in a piping voice said, "But I love Jesus, so I put flowers before His picture."

CHAPTER XV

"Ham It Up"

ONE MORNING I TOOK the Bishop of Honolulu, the Most Reverend James J. Sweeney, to the office of the Commander in Chief for a brief call on Admiral Chester W. Nimitz. The Admiral then had an office in the submarine base of the Navy Yard. As things at that moment were "popping" in the South Pacific, it was encouraging to find the Admiral looking superbly fit "for a fight or a frolic." He has remarkable poise, but that morning when he discussed the Japanese situation in Hawaii with Bishop Sweeney, it did not seem that he had the most important job west of the Mississippi.

In the corridor as we left, I noticed Rear Admiral Richard E. Byrd heading toward the office of the chief of staff. He was one of the many celebrities who, in those days, arrived unheralded and left in secret for points unknown. The next morning as I was walking down the stairway of the headquarters building, I nearly collided with Rear Admiral Thomas C. Kinkaid, whose blue uniform signified that he had just arrived from the mainland by plane. He was formerly skipper of the *Indianapolis* when I reported aboard in 1938. He came from Rome where, for over two years, he had been naval attaché, and he now had orders to take command of a task force in the

Pacific. Admiral Kinkaid was later decorated for distinguished leadership in combat with the Jap fleet.

Many new faces appeared in Honolulu in late December of 1941. Among the first to come to the Pacific Club was Jim Kilgallen who represented the International News Service. Jim lived at a Club cottage with another I.N.S. man, an old resident of Honolulu, the popular Dick Haller. They were both news-hawks in the "big time" manner, but they found time to relax in the blacked-out dining room in the evening and regale us with yarns. They said little about the present. Dick always reverted to his service as an Army sergeant in France in the First World War, while Jim held us spellbound with tales about celebrities he knew intimately, such as Al Capone, top politicians, and prize fighters of the Jack Dempsey era.

I came to the Club for lunch one day and sat at a side table. Before I had time to give my order to the Japanese waiter, Dick Haller came over and said he wanted me to meet a friend. He took me to a far table to shake the hand of Robert Casey, the author of "I Can't Forget" and "Torpedo Junction." His jovial, Irish smile immediately captivated me. He said he had just arrived by plane from Alaska on an assignment as a war correspondent for the *Chicago Daily News*. Jim Kilgallen and other correspondents were also at the table. Casey asked what I had seen at Pearl Harbor. Among the stories I gave him was that of the young seaman from the Ozarks who, when the Japs came, was sitting near a machine gun on the upper deck of the battleship *Maryland*. He was writing a letter to his mother when he spied the first Jap plane swoop down over Battleship Row. Quick to see the Rising Sun marking on the fuselage, he ran to his gun. Men of the *Maryland* will tell you that he fired the gun even before he heard the call to battle stations. The boy from the Ozarks got his man and as a reward, the Commanding Officer promoted him from seaman to gunner's mate.

Robert Casey was all ears. He looked up and smiled. "That guy," said he, "was a squirrel hunter. How could he miss? They ought to put Ozark sharpshooters on every ship. If they did, the Jap dive bombers wouldn't have a chance." We saw too little of Casey, for he never missed a chance to put to sea in a task force. He saw the whole "show," as he proved in the pages of his splendid book.

On New Year's Day of 1942, I invited a few friends to the Club to help celebrate my birthday. Early in the morning, I motored to Kaneohe Bay to celebrate Mass at the air station. After Mass, I persuaded Chief Boatswain Pat Byrne to return with me and join my dinner guests. The famous big-boat pilot had lately arrived in a PBY squadron that was summoned from Iceland on the day of the blitz. For months, my old friend Pat had seen nothing but ice, snow and the stormy North Atlantic. All the way over the mountain, he raved about the luxuriant foliage and the flowers. I had never run across such genuine enthusiasm for tropical verdure. Pat said he was well repaid for the dismal months he had spent in bleak Iceland.

I had originally planned a little family birthday dinner with the John Kangeters, Marjorie Fitzgerald and Doris Hamilton. Their husbands had sailed for the mainland. But later on, Doris suggested I invite the two correspondents and authors, H. R. Knickerbocker and Edward Amsley. Finally I corraled Commander Charlie Rend and Fathers Tom Odlum and John Wolach. The latter, a few months later, won distinction as the chaplain of Midway during the important battle of June 1942.

We sat at a huge round table in the main dining room and had great fun trying to keep the conversational pace set by "Knick" and "Eddie." At dinner, Marjorie Fitzgerald told us of the Pearl Harbor doings of her husband, Bill Fitzgerald, who later became a captain and chief of staff of the Commander of Destroyers, Pacific Fleet. We had been close friends for many years, having served together in Turkish waters and later on the China station. On December 7th, he was aide and flag secretary to Rear Admiral Walter S. Anderson, Commander Battleship Battle Force. He was staff duty officer that day and he was having breakfast a little before 8 A.M. with the chief of staff, Captain W.R. "Nick" Carter. A letter from Fitzgerald which recently came to me tells what happened.

When Nick and I arrived on the flag bridge we saw that not much could be accomplished at that station. We split up and went to the gun batteries, Nick taking the starboard AA battery and I taking the port. Naturally all hell was breaking loose and utter confusion reigned throughout. We did our best to get things squared away, including organizing ammunition parties, gun crews, assigning men to various guns, etc. There was a shortage of men on one of the guns of the port battery so for a few loads I gave them a hand as a loader. In the meantime the *Oklahoma* capsized right in front of me and that meant some more details to assist the lads in the water. Then when they were dragged aboard I further assigned them to the *Maryland* guns. When the regular battery officers had arrived and were shaken down, I returned to the flag bridge—and I assume Nick had been doing the same as I because he arrived about the same time.

That evening I had dinner with the jovial Amsley and the more analytical "strawberry blonde" Knickerbocker, both brilliant members of the fourth estate, at the Royal

Hawaiian. Bob Casey later joined us and helped materially to make it a very profitable evening.

Early one morning, my yoeman Joe Workman telephoned that Commander John Ford had just arrived at Honolulu on a transport and that my old friend was anxious to see me. When I first met Hollywood's best director in Manila in 1930, I thought his name was Forbes. That's the way it sounded when George O'Brien introduced me. I still call him Forbes because it reminds us of far happier days.

A ship that formerly came to Honolulu with gay tourists from the mainland, early one morning made fast to the pier near the Aloha Tower without benefit of the Royal Hawaiian Band, streamers or carnation leis. Her topside was drab in war paint and her compartments bulged with thousands of bluejackets. The senior naval officer among the passengers and officially in charge of them was Commander John Ford, U.S.N.R., and under his immediate command were Lieutenant Gregg Toland, U.S.N.R. and a large group of experts of the Hollywood "industry." They were a section of the large photographic unit which Ford had organized, and they had given up high paying jobs to join the Navy.

As I was leaving my quarters for the office, Commander Ford drove up the Club driveway. He had with him his "man Friday," the capable ex-Marine, Chief Boatswain Jack Pennick. Ford had come to Hawaii to make a picture. But there were countless things to attend to, so John persuaded me to join his outfit temporarily as a guide. I returned to the transport with them and stayed on board for lunch. We later drove to the Navy Yard where the officers of the unit presented their orders.

After a call on the chief of staff of the district, Captain
John W. Lewis, I took Ford to Admiral Nimitz, the Commander in Chief. Ford said that he came from the office
of the director of War Information, Colonel William
Donovan, on orders from the Secretary of the Navy, to
make a full-length motion picture of Hawaii before and
after the raid, emphasizing, of course, the battle of December 7th. He received from the Admiral *carte blanche*
to take his cameramen anywhere in the Islands, in the
Navy Yard and on board the combatant ships. We then
called on Admiral Pye and his chief of staff, Captain
Harold Train. On that particular stop on our interesting
Odyssey, the Admiral directed me to give all the time I
could spare to assisting Ford during the early days of
laying the ground work. Among the many calls that John
thought it well to make was one upon Governor Poin-
dexter. We went to his office one afternoon and had a
pleasant chat with the head of the Territorial Government. Ford also paid his respects to the Most Reverend
Bishop James J. Sweeney.

To make such a picture in face of the many restrictions
attaching to war regulations in Hawaii, it was necessary
that many passes be issued to the personnel of Ford's
photographic unit. At last they were free to move over
the Island of Oahu at will, night and day, where even
"angels feared to tread."

One afternoon before the cameras began to roll, I took
Ford and Jack Pennick on a tour of Pearl Harbor in a
staff motor-boat and gave them a "close up" of a scene of
destruction such as few have ever witnessed. As we slowly
passed the *California*, which was resting on the bottom,
her decks awash and her superstructure bent and twisted,
the tall, husky Pennick suddenly stood up in the boat

and saluted. Ford and I immediately followed him. Tears streamed down the cheeks of the rugged Pennick. He had served on board the *California* as a marine. Not a word was spoken on that slow trip down Battleship Row. Those ships were still the tombs of over two thousand young American boys. The 29,000-ton dreadnaught *Oklahoma* which turned a half-somersault and rested bottom-up, looked like the back of a gigantic whale. She held the bones of 1,509 men. Astern of her, the *West Virginia*, one of the "big five," her decks awash with huge holes torn in her port side, also rested on the bottom. The last ship in line, the *Arizona*, was broken in two, completely demolished. No wonder that scene brought tears to the eyes of a veteran leatherneck of the Marine Corps.

I shall always remember a dinner party John Ford's enlisted men gave for Father Odlum and me in their Waikiki apartment. Jack Pennick was there and Paul Moen and Braggins. Chief Hilson cooked the dinner, and it was, as the boys say, a "honey."

As technical assistant to the winner of many "Oscars," my activities were centered on a routine involving a military field Mass which someone imagined as taking place near an air station the morning of December 7th. One day when Ford was at sea in a task force, Gregg Toland and I called at the newly built Army camp at Ulupau. He needed a tent, so I described the one I had been using in the open field for hearing confessions before I offered Mass on a rough-hewn platform under the blue sky. The commanding officer, Colonel Gallagher, who came every Sunday to kneel in the tall grass with five hundred of his men, offered Gregg the tent and ordered his truck driver to take it to the air station on the shore of Kaneohe Bay. Ford and Toland had chosen a spot in a grove of palm trees where the "Mass" was to be "celebrated."

On a particularly warm Sunday when a full morning of two Masses rather tired me, I was asked to meet Ford and his gang at noon at the officer's mess on the air station. After lunch, which I rightly called breakfast, we motored to the "location." Toland broke out a church pennant which he had ordered specially made in town and hoisted it above the ensign near the tent. Young Joe Workman had rigged for church with the altar just inside the flaps. Then in the hearing of six hundred sailors and several officers, Joe argued with the ace director of the film capital as to the proper place for the altar. Joe held out for the interior of the tent and to our amusement and certainly to that of the smiling John Ford, he won the argument.

Facing the terrifying sound-recording machines and the inevitable battery of cameras commanded by Toland, considered by Ford "the best cameramen in Hollywood," at eight bells in the afternoon watch the show began.

Dog tired and with a brain benumbed by sheer fatigue, I gave the men a simple talk about the coming festival of Christmas. Ford interrupted, "That's fine, Padre, let's do it again." I was so fagged out that I forgot what I had said.

I "ad libbed" again and again until the director was satisfied. Then came the climax. I saw a man on a roof of a near-by shed wave a stick with a rag tied to it. I shouted, "To your battle stations, men—and God bless you." Pennick's sailors and aviators ran in all directions. I wheeled around and quickly removed the chasuble. The Japs had come. It was again December 7th.

A few days after John Ford came to Honolulu, the movie theatre at Waikiki ran his latest Academy Award picture, "How Green Was My Valley." John bought out the house and filled it with sailors ashore on liberty. The happy audience included many patients from the Naval Hospital. After much persuasion, I managed to get the modest Ford on the stage where he made a graceful speech, and the men gave him a "big hand."

When Monsignor Michael J. Ready, the General Secretary of the National Catholic Welfare Conference, cabled me in April an invitation to give a "Report to Mothers and Fathers" on the Catholic Hour, I told Ford that I was proud to have at last made the "big time." He will never know how he encouraged me by saying, "Nice going. I'd like to hear you read it before you go on the air."

A few nights later he came to my cottage and I broke out the script. I began to read and felt I was doing famously until he suddenly shouted, "Ham it up—ham it up." I was not sure I knew exactly what he meant until he stood in the center of the grass rug and convinced me that I was not sufficiently dramatic. He was patient with me, lavishing a million dollars worth of direction. There are not many Navy sky pilots who can boast of such topside tutelage.

This was my first broadcast over a national hook-up and I admit the thought of it gave me many uneasy moments. The hour of the broadcast was 12:30 P.M. Rather than risk the hazards of a long motor trip to Kaneohe Bay, I arranged to offer Mass at ten o'clock in the cathedral that Sunday morning. At noon I drove to the studio where I found my old friend Chaplain Razzie Truitt standing by to lend moral support. It felt good to have him there and it softened the cold defiance of the "mike."

I came through the ordeal unscathed and happy. A few months later, I learned that my address was printed in the Congressional Record. This amazing fact and the heap of fan mail made me believe I had not done badly.

One night John Ford came to the Club for dinner, joining me and two other guests, the Navy priests, Fathers Tom Odlum and John Wolach. Later, as we sat in my room, I said to Ford, "Jack, would you like to see my Pearl Harbor vestments? They floated for days in the oily and bloody waters."

He quietly examined the stained set of purple which the Chefoo orphans had made in the late twenties. He asked, "What do you intend to do with them?"

I said, "Burn them, of course."

"No," he complained. "You can't do that—they're too valuable. Think where they've been."

"Very well," I said. "Would you like to have this?" I handed him the blackened stole which had survived many Lenten seasons in the fleet.

It pleased me greatly the day John Ford returned from a flight to Washington and told me that he had given it to Colonel William Donovan who said he would present it to the "Fighting 69th" Armory in New York. Who knows? It may be there today among the trophies of that legendary regiment of valiant Irish-Americans.

CHAPTER XVI

A Gallant Admiral

In Honolulu in the summer of 1942 at dusk just before the blackout, two naval officers came to my cottage at the Pacific Club. I can still see my friends as they crossed the lawn. The younger officer was a bit taller than his companion, but both were broad-shouldered and strikingly martial as they approached and greeted me jovially in the half-light of my lanai.

They were Captain Daniel J. Callaghan and his son Judson, then an ensign. They came that evening to bid me good-by, for they had heard that my orders had arrived directing me to take passage for a tour of duty on the mainland. Father and son had dined alone that evening for they, too, were soon to be separated—Judson, the former end of the California Rose Bowl team, to board his "PT" boat for the battle of Midway, his father to board a bomber for a flight to New Zealand, where he was to assume his new duties as chief of staff of the Commander Naval Forces in the South Pacific. In a few weeks, the Captain was promoted to the rank of rear admiral.

My old friend and shipmate, Dan Callaghan, then explained this surprise return to Honolulu. For the past year he had commanded the heavy cruiser *San Francisco*, a ship named for the city of his birth. I knew that the ship had sailed for a west-coast navy yard for a period of overhaul. The day she arrived in port, dispatch orders came ordering the Captain detached, and directing him to board a clipper to Pearl Harbor and to proceed from there to his new post in the South Seas. When I congratulated my old friend on his splendid assignment, he said, "Well, Padre, it's a good job, but I hated to leave the *San Francisco*. She has the finest ship's company I have ever known. My chief regret is that I never had a chance to come to grips with the Japs. We fired the anti-aircraft guns and hit the target, but I never had a chance to fire the main battery."

The epic story of Admiral Callaghan's flagship, the *San Francisco*, which he had joined ten days before his last battle, told how Dan had attained his wish. His flagship, while leading a victorious task force against a superior concentration of enemy ships near Guadalcanal, steamed fast through the Jap fleet and fired the eight-inch guns, sinking two cruisers and crippling a big battleship. The Admiral was killed where he stood on the flag bridge. Death came to a great officer and a true gentleman.

I first met Dan twenty-two years ago when he reported for duty on board the battleship *Idaho* as assistant gunnery officer. We at once became fast friends. Our favorite pastime after working hours was to play "catch" on the spacious quarter-deck of the ship. Dan, an enthusiastic ball-player, had starred at the Naval Academy as a catcher on the varsity.

When the fleet dropped anchor off Panama in the winter of 1921, the Commander in Chief appointed Dan as playing-manager of the Pacific Fleet officers' team when they played the officers of the Atlantic Fleet. Dan played a fine game that day, and his team won. He was as happy

as a school-boy that evening at dinner in the Union Club
when we talked about it.

Dan, though invariably cheerful, was a rather quiet
fellow. He was never spectacular, but in a serene sort of
way, he was sociable. On parties, while enjoying his
inevitable glass of ginger ale, he contributed his share of
the merriment. He was ever a "grand fellow to have
around." He was notoriously a hard worker, and whatever he did, he undertook with intense enthusiasm. I believe the trait in his character which most endeared him
to his fellow officers was his code of never speaking ill of
his fellow man. He was one of the most genuinely charitable men I have ever met in the service. When Dan was
in the wardroom, you seldom heard anything said that
might injure the sensibilities of a shipmate. I have never
heard him criticize a superior officer. His very presence
commanded respect and kept his less self-disciplined shipmates under pleasing restraint.

Dan frequently came to my room aboard the *Idaho*.
He was especially fond of candy, and I managed selfishly
to keep him well supplied for fear he might choose some
other place to relax and "shoot the breeze." On the long
cruises, he spoke often of Mary, his charming wife, and
of Jud who then was but a child. The enlisted men of the
ship admired him and they were outspoken in their affection for him.

On the cruise to Valparaiso, Chile, in 1921, Dan's popu-
larity paid him a boomerang in dividends. When the ship
arrived at the equator, our assistant gunnery officer had
to undergo far rougher treatment than the rest of us in
the ceremony of making "shellbacks" out of "pollywogs"
in honor of King Neptune. I still have a snapshot of Dan,
taken when he finally managed to climb out of the jerry-

rigged tank, having been soundly spanked and roughly handled by the Royal Polar Bears. He was so "black and blue" that I found it hard to explain that this strange treatment was due to the affection the sailors felt for him and that they chose this rugged way of showing it. They knew that Dan could "take it."

Although Dan and I were shipmates only once in the early twenties, our paths among the waves frequently crossed through the years. We served again in the fleet in 1938 when Dan was on the staff of Rear Admiral Joseph K. Taussig in the flagship *Chicago*. In those days, I was scouting force chaplain, serving on the staff of Vice Admiral Adolphus Andrews on the *Indianapolis*.

On many occasions, in the evening, we met on the landing at Long Beach and motored to Los Angeles for a quiet dinner. We once made a trip to Westwood Village on a house-hunting expedition. Dan had been told that he would soon be ordered to establish the Reserve Officers' Training Corps at the University of California in Los Angeles. He had enjoyed similar duty at Berkeley. It was the sort of shore duty he liked because it meant a summer cruise with the embryo officers.

A few weeks later I drove my friend to the Biltmore Hotel where he was to meet Mary, his wife. It was dinnertime. When he arrived in the lobby, he discovered a bellhop was paging him. He was wanted at the telephone. "The White House is calling Captain Daniel J. Callaghan." At first Dan thought it was a joke, but he soon learned that President Franklin Delano Roosevelt had chosen him to be his naval aide.

Although Dan Callaghan was handsome and always well-groomed, I never thought that he would particularly enjoy that sort of duty. He was more in his natural element aboard ship, training officers and men in gunnery. The prime purpose of the Navy's fighting ship had shaped his career. He was essentially a sea-going officer, but I was not surprised to learn that he was highly successful as a presidential aide; and it is apparent that the President quickly discovered Dan's sterling qualities, for Dan was a man after his own heart.

When his tour as President's aide came to an end, Dan took command of the heavy cruiser *San Francisco* at Pearl Harbor in the summer of 1941. He was again back in the world he loved.

At that time, I was fleet chaplain of the Pacific Fleet. One day Captain Callaghan came to my office in Honolulu. He was noticeably sad. I had not seen that expression on his face for years. He came to my desk and quietly said: "Padre, one of my men was washed over the side last week in a storm at sea. I'd like to have you conduct a memorial service for him. He was a fine kid, one of my leading bo'sun's mates, and I feel badly about it."

The following Sunday, I went aboard the *San Francisco*, and found the skipper personally supervising the arrangements. The whole ship's company, excepting those on watch, assembled on the well-deck and attended the Mass I offered in the airplane hangar. It was typical of Dan Callaghan to make the long trip from Pearl Harbor to the city and to attend personally to all the details of this service in honor of one of his men lost in line of duty.

One morning last May, when I discovered that the *San Francisco* had come to Pearl Harbor for minor repairs following the battle of the Coral Sea, I called on the skipper, and we chatted at length in his cabin. Dan said, "I've got a great crew, Padre. The ship has been seventy-five days at sea and the food had to be rationed, and the men joked about the turkey they didn't get. A few nights ago, while on the bridge, I heard the men singing in the darkness of the boat-deck. Their voices became louder and then so loud that I was tempted to order them to 'pipe down.' I couldn't hear myself think but I let them sing until they got so tired they turned in. They have marvelous spirit. They are the finest men I have ever known."

Dan Callaghan thought of these things as he sat on my lanai at the Pacific Club. He regretted that he had not fired his main battery at the enemy, not realizing that he had always fired, as it were, the main battery in everything he had ever undertaken to do. The last sight that met the eyes of Dan Callaghan, as he viewed at night the ships of the enemy's battle line, was the flashing salvos of the main battery of his beloved *San Francisco*.

The Navy, in November 1942, ordered me to San Francisco to offer a Solemn Mass of Requiem in St. Mary's Cathedral for Rear Admiral Callaghan. The Most Reverend John J. Mitty, Archbishop of San Francisco, presided. Naval Academy classmates, officers and men of the fleet and civilians who knew Dan as a boy at St. Ignatius College, came to pay last tribute to their hero-friend.

My old friend, Father George A. O'Meara, a pastor in San Rafael, California, and for over fifteen years the Catholic chaplain at San Quentin prison, on request of the Archbishop, preached the eulogy at Admiral Callaghan's Requiem Mass. He telephoned me from San Rafael and asked me whether I had a thought or two for his sermon which indeed was a masterpiece. The first idea that came to me was Dan's regret that he had never had a chance to fire the *San Francisco's* main battery of eight-inch guns at the enemy. Father George grasped it with hooks of steel and skillfully adapted it to his well-written sermon. I have in my files a copy of Father O'Meara's eulogy. In part he said: "We ask today God's mercy for one who went down often to the sea in ships; and who finally had the glory of standing on the bridge of his favorite ship, and of defending her even unto death. We need not eulogize him. . . . Here was a good father, a devoted husband, a genuine friend, a loyal Catholic and a great sailor. We who are fighting today against paganism, may well take an example from Admiral Daniel Callaghan. . . . The story of this courageous officer will be an inspiration to bluejackets as well as to the seasoned officers of the line, to give their all to keep flying high the Stars and Stripes. It will make them true to Cross and Flag."

In the spring of 1943, I received a letter from Captain William M. Callaghan, Dan's brother who is now serving on the staff of the Commander in Chief of the Pacific Fleet. He said:

Dan's death was a terrible blow to me and to all of us. I had seen him just about five weeks before when I made the trip south with the Admiral. He looked awfully tired and worn out then, for, as you well know, both Admiral Ghormley and himself had been carrying a crushing load for quite some time. Our hold on Guadalcanal was precarious and our reserve strength appeared none too ample to meet the hard blows which the Japs were expected to and finally did make. One of the incidents I like to recall in connection with that last visit was typical of Dan's never-failing consideration for his shipmates.

One of the senior officers on the staff had been in ill health for some time and was only being retained by Admiral Ghormley because of the critical need for a man of his talents and experience. In order to spare him and give him as much comfort as possible, Dan had insisted that he take his nice, comfortable bed every night while Dan slept on a cot in the office adjoining his cabin. It was a small thing for Dan to make that sacrifice but so indicative of the big heart he had wherever his friends or anyone in need were concerned.

A great naval officer, a great gentleman, has given his life for victory. His career is now part of the magnificent tradition of the United States Navy.

CHAPTER XVII

Padres

HAVING AN OFFICE in the Army and Navy "Y," which is in the very center of Honolulu, gave me a good chance to keep in touch with the chaplains who were serving afloat. It was next to impossible to learn when they were coming or going, so I depended on their paying me surprise visits when their ships came to Pearl Harbor. They seldom told you where they had been or what they had done to the Japs but you could always count on picking up information about mutual friends, especially fellow chaplains.

It became obvious that Father Lawrence R. Schmieder's heavy cruiser was making runs "down under." He was always away for such long periods that I knew he had convoyed ships to Australia.

Father Larry seemed to be quite unaffected by the long cruises at sea. He still retained his engaging smile and infectious enthusiasm and when he appeared on the club tennis courts, he stepped around like a young colt as though playing tennis had been his daily form of amusement.

It was always refreshing to chat with Father Ozias B. Cook when his big flat-top returned with a task force. He was proud of his shipmates, especially the aviators, and told many stories of their heroism and will to win.

For many reasons, I was particularly interested in getting news about our chaplains who were serving in the Asiatic Fleet when the war began. The fleet chaplain in the Far East was my friend, Captain George S. Rentz. We had served together when I was on the China station in 1929 and I knew Mrs. Rentz and the children quite well. George was universally admired by officers and men. He was on board the *Houston* during the battle of the Java Sea and everyone hoped he had been rescued. Many months passed before it was officially announced that he had been killed in action.

I shall always remember gratefully how kind he was in 1931 when he offered his help in getting out a souvenir book on the East Indies cruise of the *Pittsburgh*. While I gathered information and pictures for the book and sent them by air mail from Singapore, Batavia and Makassar, Rentz, in Manila, rushed the copy to the printer and, by using nightly radiograms, we edited the material and had the finished book on the dock when the *Pittsburgh* returned to Manila. We enjoyed many a laugh over it. George never quite realized how he had saved the day.

Many have asked me whether I knew the circumstances of Chaplain Thomas L. Kirkpatrick's death. He was on board the *Arizona* when the Japs destroyed her at Pearl Harbor. I made extensive inquiries among the *Arizona* survivors to no avail. Apparently my Protestant colleague, who was slated to relieve me as fleet chaplain, was killed when an aerial bomb struck the ship's magazines and caused great loss of life. My friend Tom had made an outstanding record in the chaplain corps. His death was a heavy blow to those who knew his sterling virtues.

The only news I received of Father Francis J. Mac-Manus whose ship, the *Canopus*, was lost near Cavite,

P. I., came from Lieutenant Robert B. Kelly of the famous "Expendables." I met Kelly in the fall of 1942 at a luncheon in New York. He said he had seen Father Mac-Manus on Bataan serving with a battalion of bluejackets. It has also been reported that he is a prisoner. The last time I saw Frank was when he spent a few hours with me in the spring of 1940 in Honolulu when he was on his way to Manila. I met him at the pier and drove him to the Pacific Club. Under his arm was a package which aroused my curiosity. On the way to the club he said, "Mac, do you remember telling me once that you hoped some day to have a crucifix carved in Oberammergau? Well, here's one I picked up one summer when I was on vacation. I want you to have it." Father MacManus had studied for the priesthood in Innsbruck, Austria, and he had a liking for the finer things. It is a really fine piece of carving which I luckily carried ashore from the *California* a few days before the Jap raid. It is an appropriate memento of my brave but unfortunate friend.

My cottage at the Pacific Club also became a happy rendezvous for the chaplains. It was always an especial treat to have Stanton Salisbury of the *Pennsylvania*, Bob Leonard, or Bart Stephens of the *Maryland* come by for dinner or for an evening chat on the lanai. They are among the old-timers of the corps. The younger fellows came too and I shall always remember how happy we were to have Father Aloysius H. Schmitt join us on our occasional "soirées." He was tall, slender, and he looked no older than his age. He had all the ear-marks of a young junior officer fresh from the "Navy School at Crab Town." It was only after he plunged into a heated argument over a point in canon law that we realized he had made a fine record as a student at the North American College in

Rome. He entered the Navy as a priest of the diocese of Dubuque, Iowa, and his first assignment as a chaplain was to the battleship *Oklahoma*.

I recall an evening in Long Beach, California, when Father Walter Mahler and I stood on the Navy landing waiting for a boat to take us to our ships. A lieutenant commander came up and said, "When is Father Schmitt coming back? The *Oklahoma* hasn't been the same since he left. We're all keen for him."

He then told us that the padre was a patient in the San Diego Naval Hospital. A few days later, Father John Murphy and I motored down the coast and found our friend moving heaven and earth to get back to his ship.

Later in Honolulu, when I had the job of allocating invitations to large parties of shore-going bluejackets, we always counted on the *Oklahoma* men to attend because Father Al carefully rounded up the sailors and usually accompanied them on our picnics and beach parties. Whenever he came to Honolulu, he called at my office seeking invitations for his shipmates. He was proud of the *Oklahoma* crew and it is quite natural that the men loved the young padre.

A few days after the Pearl Harbor raid, two chaplains came ashore to dine with me at the Pacific Club. They were Father Schmieder and Father Cook. We later sat in my room and "shot the breeze." Their ships were at sea on December 7th, so they were hungry for news about our personnel casualties. They were especially anxious that I tell them all I knew about the circumstances of Father Schmitt's death.

They spoke in highest terms of their colleague, recalling his youthful way of revealing a sunny disposition. They referred to his scholarly attainments—how he modestly showed he "knew the answers"—and they were deeply affected by the grim fact that he was no longer one of us in the corps of chaplains. I found myself again telling how the Jap planes dropped their torpedoes which pierced the side of the *Oklahoma* and killed that great ship by destroying the hundreds of men who had made her vibrant with life. I told them of the many tales I had heard of Father Schmitt's heroic self-sacrifice at the end. I told them of searching for an eye-witness of our friend's last hour and showed them a letter I had received that very day, a letter from W. A. Perrett, an electrician's mate, first class, who had, with his own hands, struggled to save the life of the beloved padre of the *Oklahoma*.

Here is the letter I read that night to my friends:

DEAR CHAPLAIN MAGUIRE:

In answer to your letter of January 31, 1942, the following is respectfully submitted.

On the morning of December 7, 1941, before the Japanese raid on Pearl Harbor area, I was on board the U.S.S. *Oklahoma*. The day before I had put in an early call for Sunday morning.

I left the work-shop at 0715 for the mess casemate on the superstructure deck. Passing by the crew's recreation room, I saw Chaplain Schmitt holding early Sunday Mass as he usually did every Sunday. I did not see him again until after the raid had started. The Japs caught most of us at our working stations. We then went to our battle stations. Mine was on the third deck. Somehow, I got to the second deck. I saw aft to the first vacant porthole and pulled myself through with the help from my ship-mates on the outside. Men were helping each other get out for no other way of escape could be found—every man did all he could to help his shipmates.

The ship was listing from 20° to 25° when I was pulled through the port. At that moment, I heard someone yelling.

Looking around, I recognized Chaplain Schmitt. He said, "Boys, I'm having a tough time getting through." So we all got together and tried to pull him out. But no luck.

His next words really took the three of us by surprise, and will linger with us for some time. "Men, you are endangering your lives, and I'm keeping others from getting through." But we tried again to pull him out.

One of the men said, "Chaplain, if you go back in there, you'll never come out."

Then Father Schmitt said, "Please let go of me, and may God bless you all." He disappeared back in the ship knowing well that he would never come out of it alive. The ship was slowly turning over.

Four or five men came out of that port while I was there helping. Soon we had to leave. It was getting too hot to stick around.

We left the *Oklahoma* by jumping into the sea and swam towards the U.S.S. *Maryland* where we were hoisted aboard. A few minutes later, the ship turned turtle and with her went a brave and courageous man, a man who gave his life in keeping with the best traditions of the U. S. Navy.

Another sailor who tried with electrician Perrett to save the life of Father Schmitt, said, "When Father Schmitt told us to save ourselves and to push him back so others could escape through the port, it broke my heart. I could hear him splash in the water but I couldn't see him—it was too dark."

A Navy ship now bears the name of Aloysius H. Schmitt. May she always be worthy of her name.

CHAPTER XVIII

"Keep the Faith"

SINCE THAT DREADFUL December day when the American people accepted the Axis challenge to fight in defense of life's greatest blessings, men of the armed forces have acquired a new appreciation of the little things which help us to walk with God.

When I see a sailor wearing a blessed medal on a chain, I feel that he carries with him a reminder of his Faith and a sign for others to see that he recognizes as his Eternal Commander in Chief—Christ the King. It also reminds me of my student days in Belgium and vacation time when I visited friends in their homes.

It was customary for us American seminarians on the long vacations to choose a country for the purpose of acquiring a working knowledge of a foreign language. My classmates scattered to the four winds. It depended on the sort of missionary work they intended to do after their ordination and return to the United States. One of my fellow Americans spent his summers in Russia because his bishop had in mind a parish in which a knowledge of Russian would be of value in the pulpit and confessional. Others went to Germany, Italy and France for the same purpose. For the most part, I divided the vacation months between Germany and Switzerland with, I confess, a special regard for the scenery.

We also made it a point to seek quarters in the home of the local pastor. This gave us a chance to meet and to know many delightful people of the parish. They invited us to their homes and took us off on family picnics. After a day in the woods in Belgium or France, when the moment of parting came, our friends always said good-by by adding, "*Gardez la foi,*" meaning "Keep the Faith." It was old-fashioned and delightfully Catholic.

In December, 1941, Bishop James J. Sweeney asked me to write for his *Catholic Herald* a weekly column, a sermonette, as it were, and I drew upon my years in the Navy for appropriate anecdotes to illustrate a moral lesson. Father Speer Strahan, the poet, then serving as an Army chaplain in Hawaii, was also a contributor. While I was laboriously typing one night in the ill-ventilated "blackout" bedroom of my cottage at the Pacific Club, Commander John Kangeter telephoned me from his home on Pacific Heights. It was most likely an invitation to dine. In any case, he asked me what I was up to at the moment and I told him, "I'm writing a piece for the *Herald* on 'Keep the Faith.' "

He exclaimed, "Splendid." And then with spirit, he went on, "We need it. Be sure to mention along with faith in God—faith in our country, our constitution, our leaders in Church and State, the Army and Navy—faith in our national destiny."

I admired John's enthusiasm, being certain of his sincerity, for I had long known that he and his exemplary wife and children were "keeping the faith" commendably.

I went back to the typewriter and continued, "I have since cherished the memory of that parting salutation, '*Gardez la foi*' as a truly Christian 'Aloha.' What my European friends meant was, 'Be a soldier of Christ; stand steadfast against the attacks of false prophets and their works.' If an American keeps the faith of his fathers, he will have faith in his country and its government because, for the most part, our American way of life was founded on the principles laid down by our Savior Jesus Christ.

"The Bill of Rights, that great guarantee of freedom of speech and worship, proved a boon to the unhappy peoples of the Old Country. It made the United States the haven of security and happiness. Millions of victims of famine, tyranny and wars came to our shores where the weak and humble were welcomed; where the ambitious and strong were encouraged; where they found reason to have Faith in the Constitution." Thus with the aid of my officer friend, I was able to "make the dead-line" for the Honolulu *Catholic Herald*.

Evidence of practical faith in the religion of Christ, and reverence for all that implies, whether expressed by friends or by people we meet in the market place, I find encouraging. I recall a story told many years ago by the late Monsignor Jules de Becker, the rector of our seminary in Belgium. He told of dining one evening in Washington in the home of Chief Justice White of the Supreme Court. Being an exemplary Catholic, the host treated our rector with appropriate deference. When it came time to leave, the distinguished jurist insisted that he help his guest get into his heavy overcoat. Against the Monsignor's protest, the aged Chief Justice gave an excellent imitation of a Pullman porter. It was a story with a point to it. Here was a famous man holding a position to which every good lawyer aspires, showing humility, kindness and above all the respect for Holy Orders and the dignity of an ambassador of Christ.

It is a custom in the wardrooms of our ships, should an officer become overly tensed and let slip an expression that may be offensive to a Christian's sensibilities, for him to say, "I beg your pardon, Padre." It is simply a way of showing he recognizes the chaplain's sacred mission.

When Brest, France, was a great American naval base in 1918, a signalman standing on the bridge of the battleship *Virginia* semaphored a message to my ship, the destroyer-tender *Prometheus*. It was New Year's Eve. The message read, "Commanding Officer is on the sick list. Request chaplain bring him Holy Communion in the morning."

Boarding a boat soon after reveille the next day, I sped across the inner harbor and drew up alongside the old "iron-clad." A few yards ahead of the gangway stood a huge coal barge and on top of its black and dusty cargo, briskly wielding their shovels, were members of the crew. Coaling ship was an "all hands evolution." For them, this was no holiday and no one went to Holy Mass that morning. When I arrived, the *Virginia* was the busiest and noisiest spot on the face of the globe. Sailing orders called for immediate departure after coaling.

As the motor-boat came to a stop at the gangway and the bowman made fast with his line, I heard the officer of the deck on topside give an order, "Bosun's mate. Pass the word: 'all hands knock off coaling.'" Then the reply, "Aye, aye, Sir."

By the time I reached the deck, ever conscious that I was carrying the Blessed Sacrament in my blouse pocket, the men down in the coal barge were leaning on their shovels and standing in silence. Some of them, seeing the silver cross on the collar of my blouse, guessed why I was there at that early hour; they doffed their woolen watch caps and reverently bowed their heads.

With what seemed an especially respectful salute, the officer of the deck greeted me as I came aboard. Side boys stood at rigid attention, and a messenger waited near by for orders to escort me to the Captain's cabin. The ship was as still as a church.

The commanding officer, the late Rear Admiral H. J. Ziegemeier, lay seriously ill in his bunk. Above him hung a crucifix, and a picture of the Madonna and Child graced the steel bulkhead. After I administered the Sacraments, the Captain's face showed there was peace and happiness in his heart. He grasped my hand and said, "Thank you, Padre—Happy New Year." The instant I reached topside, the bosun's mate again yelled down to the grimy men in the coal barge: "Now get this down there—all hands turn to—and COAL SHIP!" The men of the battleship had made a good start on the course of a new and better year.

One of my friends, a destroyer skipper, wears on a chain a St. Christopher medal wrought in gold. It was originally mine but I gave it to him the night before he sailed on a perilous mission against the Japs. When he returned from a successful raid on the enemy's island bases in the South Pacific, he came to have dinner with me. Later in the evening when he was telling me how admirably his sailors had fought the guns and how proud he was of their performance, I interrupted him by saying, "By the way, Charlie, are you wearing the St. Christopher medal?"

He placed his hand on his breast where the medal hung and smilingly replied, "This, my good Padre, made the difference between a hit and a near miss." He then told how an enemy bomb, hurtling from an opening in the clouds, had landed fearfully close to the ship and the three hundred men of his command.

A few weeks later when the destroyer acquired a new mast, the Captain discovered nickels and dimes and pennies—all "heads up"—under the step of the old one. He was not surprised because when the time comes to step the mast of a new ship, there is always someone present who recalls the old superstition and gets appropriately busy with small change. This sea custom dates back to the days of pagan Rome. Builders of ships in ancient times placed coins of varied importance at the step or bottom of the mast. They believed that if a ship met disaster at sea, the coins would serve as payment to Charon for a ferry ride for all hands across the river Styx. This old superstition persists in our own Navy. It is recorded that when the heavy cruiser *New Orleans* was being built, ten pennies were placed beneath the foremast, and two dimes, three nickels and twenty-eight pennies were placed under the step of the mainmast—"heads up."

When the time came to step the new mast, the skipper remembered the ancient custom. He sent a bluejacket to a near-by ship to ask the priest chaplain for a holy medal. When the sailor returned, the Captain knelt at the spot where the mast was to be placed and made a circle of the coins he had found there, and in the center he laid a Miraculous Medal of the Blessed Virgin Mary. He offered a prayer that the Mother of God might, by her unfailing intercession, guide and protect his ship and his valiant crew.

I have found great faith in the men of the Navy and I

sometimes think how fine it would be, when we salute our comrades in arms, if that military gesture of brotherhood were secretly to imply the inspiring salutation, "Keep the Faith."

CHAPTER XIX

The Prune Barge

THE MORNING THE Yard tugs helped the crippled *California* across the harbor and eased her gently into the dry dock, I motored to Pearl Harbor to view the damage done to her hull. I counted four big gaping holes in her port side; one was as wide as a ferry slip. The ship had lain on the bottom for months, and it was hard to believe that she had once been the queen of the seas, the smart and happy flagship of the battle force.

When I joined her in the Fall of 1940, Admiral Charles P. Snyder flew his four-star flag at the main. On his staff were many old friends. The force gunnery officer was Commander Jerome F. Donovan whom I had known years before in the scouting force. He often came to my room in the *California* for a chat and I as often went to his for expert advice when I faced an assignment involving unusual procedure.

Once "Jerry" reminded me of a night in Philadelphia after a Navy-Penn football game in 1932. Commander Frederick L. Riefkohl lived in the apartment next to mine. That evening, he entertained a group of Navy friends, among whom were "Jerry" and Commander "Dick" Field. I had gone to the theatre that evening and arrived home rather late, too late to join my old confrères who were still celebrating the Navy victory. I gingerly turned the key in my door and tip-toed into my room where I saw a dim light in the far corner. As I removed my overcoat, I discovered a man in full uniform sitting in a large chair. His cap was pulled down over his eyes and he seemed to be asleep. I placed my hand on his brow to arouse him but I pulled away with a muffled groan. His brow was cold as ice and I thought he was dead although his "head" dissolved into apples and his "brow" was a slice of cold bologna. In a split second I had seen flashes of newspaper head-lines, "Dead man found in chaplain's room." By the time I pulled myself together, Fritz Riefkohl's friends came in and enjoyed a hearty laugh. It didn't strike me then as being quite that funny and the shock kept me tossing in my bed the rest of the night. Jerry and Dick Field had made the course under par.

I joined the *California* with orders to assume additional duty on Admiral Snyder's staff the day before the ship sailed from Hawaii to the mainland. Chaplain Frank H. Lash, whom I relieved, stayed on board until we dropped anchor off Long Beach. I leisurely took over his many duties. In Frank's methodic way, he had the "taking over" business skillfully spaced over a week. He took me each day on tours of the ship, introducing me as we went along to the key men of the crew. We frequently dropped in on the chief petty officers for a cup of coffee. They were a jolly group and the senior member of their mess then was the famous ex-boxing champ of the Navy, and the ship's chief master-at-arms, the legendary John "Spud" Murphy. Although it is not a Navy custom to address a chief as "Mister," John Murphy rated "Mister" nonetheless from the young bluejackets because they recognized in him a sailor man who had the force and dignity of a chief of police. He was "Mr. Law" to the youngsters below decks.

They tell a story about my friend Murphy and it is attributed to Admiral James O. Richardson. I heard the yarn the first week I was aboard. The story goes that one day at sea, the Admiral was pacing the quarter-deck when a young sailor, carrying a bucket of water, went by and saluted. The Admiral stopped him. "Son," he said, "who is the commander of the Battle Force?"

The lad looked up at the tall and rugged flag officer as though he thought, "That's a cinch." He replied, "Richardson, Sir."

"Who's in command of this ship?"

The sailor knew the answer. "Bemis, Sir."

The Admiral continued his quiz. "Who is the chief master-at-arms?"

Without hesitation, the lad replied, "Mr. Murphy."

In that boy's figuring, the famous "Spud" was the only one on board who rated a "handle" on his name.

John Murphy was a good influence on the young members of the crew. He had a way, in "old Navy" fashion, of keeping the men in line by constant vigilance and a sharp wit. In the short time we were shipmates, John brought many youngsters to my room for the finishing touch after he had worked on the lad's problems in the manner of a big brother. By force of urging and good example, Murphy brought back many straying sheep to the fold. John was an exemplary Catholic and an ideal shipmate.

Among the many virtues that made the *California* crew famous in the Fleet, I believe their faithful attendance at Holy Mass and Protestant Divine Service was outstanding. Before the ship acquired a priest, the *California's* Catholic Church parties were the largest. Their fifty-foot motor launch was always filled on Sunday mornings. My friend, Chaplain Frank Lash, an Episcopalian, was beloved by the crew, and he may have been responsible for this. I recall that one of his Catholic shipmates when paid off on the *California*, entered the Trappist monastery in Kentucky—Frank had encouraged him. The Catholic men held him in high esteem; he was their friend.

It was gratifying to see so many *California* men come to daily Mass in the crew's reception room, and among them were at least a dozen communicants. John Murphy and his police petty officers maintained silence in the nearby casemates. It was an experience I shall long remember.

The *California* went to the navy yard at Bremerton, Washington, in the winter of 1940. As was our custom, we priests on the day of arrival, called on Father Joseph Camerman, the pastor of the Bremerton parish and a lieutenant commander of the Naval Reserve. One evening, we realized that there was a record number of Catholic chaplains present. The tender *Medusa* had Father Mahler. The battleship *Tennessee* was in with Father John Murphy on board, and Father Frank Burke had arrived in the *Nevada*. Early in December, we decided to hold a Solemn High Mass at midnight on Christmas Eve. Our first difficulty was to find a suitable place to accommodate the huge congregation we knew would attend. Chaplain Alfred D. Vogler saved the day by offering us the hangar deck of the carrier *Enterprise*. Her commanding officer, Captain Charles Pownall, had given his hearty approval, and we went to work on our plans. To make it officially a fleet event, I prepared a letter for the Admiral's signature which tersely outlined the details and invited all the personnel of the navy yard and the ships present to attend.

We held meetings in my room on board the *California*. When the subject of a bluejacket choir came up for discussion, Father Murphy assured us that one of his sailors would take care of that detail. Starting at scratch, the *Tennessee* "Tar" organized and trained a group of sailors that would have made good in the choir loft of any city church.

In the print shop of the *California*, a program was printed. On the front page was a cut of Raphael's Madonna and Child and inside the folded program was an English translation of the Mass. Then followed a list of those who took part. My young colleagues insisted that I be the celebrant and preacher. Father Frank Burke was deacon, Father Walter Mahler was sub-deacon and Father Jack Murphy was master-of-ceremonies.

During the afternoon of Christmas Eve, each chaplain heard confessions on his own ship and after dinner we all went to the *Enterprise* and heard confessions until 11:45 P.M. By midnight, there were more than three thousand officers, enlisted men and their families on the well-deck of the carrier. It was the most impressive ceremony of its kind I had ever seen on board a Navy ship. It was made possible through the courtesy of Captain Charles Pownall and the whole-hearted cooperation of his chaplains—both Protestants. It was typical of the spirit of friendliness I have always found in the Navy.

When a dispatch from the Commander Battle Force, who was in Hawaii, came with orders for me to take passage in the *Nevada* and to join the Admiral in Pearl Harbor, it was necessary that I turn over my collateral duties to some other officer. As aide for morale to the executive officer, I was ship's librarian, entertainment officer, and custodian of an emergency welfare fund. The commanding officer assigned as my relief, Lieutenant Henry E. Burnstein, the ship's communication officer. My friend Henry, a Jew, was extremely popular with all hands else they would not have dubbed him "Father Mac Bernstein." When the *California*, at the end of the yard overhaul, again joined the fleet, I was told of the high success Henry achieved as a pinch-hitter for the chaplain corps and I presented him with a little gold cross as a symbol in memento of his brief tour of duty as a sky-pilot.

The "Prune Barge," as the sailors called the splendid *California*, was still in a Pearl Harbor dry-dock when I sailed for the mainland in the summer of 1942. But now she is with her sister-ships on the high seas, bristling with renewed life and on the quest for sea fights and victory.

CHAPTER XX

Freight Shed

ONE NIGHT IN 1921 at an officers' smoker at the Great
Lakes Naval Training Station, the welfare officer, Lieutenant Commander Jonas H. Ingram, who is now a vice
admiral in command of a naval force in the South Atlantic,
made a speech or rather he made two speeches and both
were equally important. As welfare officer, Ingram did
not confine his activities to the recreation of the enlisted
personnel. He was just as interested in the officers' welfare and he urged them to devote at least an hour or two
a day to handball, tennis or golf. Once a month, he promoted a stag smoker for the officers in the station field
house. With ample funds that were available, he hired
entertainers to come from Chicago and stage an evening
of vaudeville. At one of the performances, Commander
Ingram said, "Gentlemen, a naval officer makes his reputation at sea, not ashore. He comes ashore mostly for a
breathing spell and a break from the confining life aboard
ship. So let's make the best of this tour of shore duty and
keep fit by taking plenty of exercise."

Jonas Ingram, since his midshipman days at Annapolis
when Walter Camp of Yale tagged him an "All American
Fullback," exemplified the meaning of the expression
"mens sana in corpore sano"—sound mind in a sound
body. As a born leader of men, he was destined to reach
commanding heights in his colorful career.

That night at Great Lakes, we gave him a high mark as an impresario. The show ran along smoothly until one of the actors, misjudging his audience, resorted to off-color stories. His first joke fell upon unresponsive ears and when he tried again, Ingram rose from his chair to make his second speech; he said, "Young fellow. We are not interested in that kind of humor. If you can't tell clean stories, you may shove off."

The comedian withdrew hastily.

The first speech of our welfare officer that evening over twenty years ago may not have influenced me to any great extent for I had a strong preference anyway for life on board Navy ships. But I believed he was right in saying that a Navy man's success should be measured by his performance afloat and not ashore. And this is particularly true of a chaplain.

Few people realize what it requires of a churchman to live day in and day out in the atmosphere of the strict discipline of a warship where everyone works, thinks and for the most part talks engineering, communications and gunnery exercises. Only the few can stick it out for long. I am not surprised although I am disappointed to reflect that for the past quarter of a century the quota for Catholic chaplains for the Navy has never been filled.

Shore duty never struck me as being quite Navy duty. If chaplains were required to serve only in navy yards and stations, I would not have remained in the service. The place for the Navy chaplain is far from home, serving officers and men on board ship.

Shore duty, however, gave me opportunities for service as a priest which I seldom enjoyed in the fleet. Although our orders to a shore station made no mention of ministering to the sick in our naval hospitals, we chaplains always considered it a matter of conscience to make daily visits to the wards. When I was on duty in Brooklyn Navy Yard with my non-Catholic friend, Chaplain Stanton W. Salisbury, we considered a daily visit to the hospital of paramount importance. Nowadays, each hospital has chaplains —Protestant, Jewish and Catholic—to give spiritual comfort to the sick. I now find it no longer necessary to make daily sick calls at the San Diego Naval Hospital as I was required to do when I served five years ago at the training station. My old friend, Father Thomas F. Regan, is now running the sick calls there, and I feel the Bureau could not have chosen a better man for the job. The Protestant patients have the full-time services of Chaplain Henry G. Gatlin. The Jews are attended by Chaplain Samuel Sandmel.

"Grady" Gatlin, since World War I, has made an enviable record in the chaplain corps. I recall chatting with him on the landing at Guantanamo Bay, Cuba, late one afternoon in 1939. Dressed in shorts and a pith helmet, it was evident he had just taken a group of *Yorktown* sailors on a hike over the sun-baked hills. He smilingly told me on our trip across the bay how much he enjoyed working with the men of the big "flat-top."

Chaplain Samuel Sandmel, a young rabbi, covers a large territory in the San Diego area. Twice a week he comes to the training station and on Sundays he holds a morning service in our North Chapel for recruits of the Jewish faith. Chaplain Sandmel is universally liked and he is certainly an asset to any command.

I first met Father "Tommy" Regan in the summer of 1917 on the landing at Yorktown, Virginia. He was then serving on board the battleship *Minnesota*. My ship was the *Maine*. We chaplains had strange collateral duties in

those days but I believe Tommy's list of varied assignments topped them all. This devotion to the men, even to
the point of enacting in and out of season the role of
Santa Claus which consumed most of his pay, won him
a warm place in the hearts of his fellow chaplains. To a
bluejacket in need of funds, Tommy could never say,
"No." Although his officer shipmates were extremely fond
of him, Father Tommy's recollections seldom take you to
the wardroom; his stories are invariably about the sailors
he has served with in home waters or on the "Far China
Station."

One of Father Regan's favorite yarns is about the
young bluejacket who rated "rat liberty." The jovial
padre told me the yarn years ago when he was attached
to the destroyer-tender *Dobbin*. The *Dobbin*, which was
a sort of floating navy yard, remained in port for long
periods, repairing the hard driven "cans." At times, you
could count seven destroyers moored alongside the famous
tender, seeking repairs, and the men sought the counsel
of their popular chaplain.

One of the problems resulting from the *Dobbin's* role
as a "pond lily" had to do with exterminating rats that
managed, in spite of metal rat-guards on the anchor chain,
to sneak aboard. The commanding officer one day thought
up a scheme to rid the ship of the rodents. He had the word
passed that for every rat a sailor killed, he would grant the
lad fifteen minutes extra liberty ashore; it was known as
"rat liberty." The chief master-at-arms kept a log for
the rat-hunters and the awards in the form of liberty,
were cumulative. It became a competitive sport.

A young, red-headed *Dobbin* sailor, whom everyone
liked, had the risky habit of always catching the last
boat to the ship. Occasionally, he missed the last one, but

his skill in finding excuses and his otherwise clear record won leniency at the captain's mast.

One morning, Father Regan went ashore on duty and discovered the sailor standing on the landing. "Son," said the padre, "do you realize you are four hours over-leave? The Old Man will sure 'hang' you this time. You'd better dig up a good alibi."

The sailor gave the chaplain a worried look, saluted, and stepped into the motor launch.

At the captain's mast the following day, the sailor came to face the music. Although the chaplain had already mentioned the man's general reputation, the skipper quickly scanned the pages of his service record and said, "Young man, you have an excellent record but you were four hours over-leave. Do you realize that this is a serious offence?"

"Yes, Sir," replied the sailor, "but the room clerk forgot to call me. I thought it was serious then, Sir, but now I don't think so."

"What's that?" exclaimed the Captain, removing his spectacles. "What changed your mind?"

"Well, Sir," replied the sailor, "I just remembered I rate four hours rat-liberty—and I'll take it now."

When I arrived in San Diego with orders to the training station, I was glad to find Father Regan in his favorite element, a hospital. On duty constantly, attending the dying at all hours of the night and patiently interviewing sailors and Marines during the day, he is making an enviable record that some day will become a legend.

The Naval Hospital at San Diego is probably the largest service hospital in the world. It stands on a hill overlooking the bay, and it has grown to enormous size since the outbreak of World War II. It was Father Regan's hope that a chapel would be included in the new construction but those in authority decided to wait until after the war is won. With characteristic enthusiasm, the padre consulted with Captain Mortimer D. Willcutts, MC, the executive officer, regarding a place that could be remodeled and made to serve as a chapel. One day he discovered a possibility in a building where freight was being stowed. What he achieved in a few weeks, became the theme of a story I recently read in the *Tidings*, the Catholic weekly of the Diocese of Los Angeles. Virginia T. Lane, who came to the hospital to sing for the patients, wrote:

"It is just a small chapel, named—appropriately enough—'Our Lady of Victory.'

"A month ago it was nothing more than a freight shed in a far corner of the great U.S. Naval Hospital in San Diego. But under the supervision of Commander Thomas F. Regan, Senior Chaplain at the hospital, it has become a thing of beauty. No matter what time of the day or night you enter, you find sailors and Marines there praying. Not all are Catholics. But all have one thing in common—suffering.

"I saw one young sailor, who had lost a leg when he was blown off his ship during the battle of the Solomons, saying the Stations. The stump-stump of his crutch echoed in the silence. A Marine flyer was saying his rosary. He could only feel the beads. He would never see them.

"After a while, two sailors came in to practice the music for the Sunday Mass. A rich baritone voice sang the 'Sanctus' from the Bach Mass. The boy had once been a singer with Paul Whiteman's orchestra.

" 'They were all happy-go-lucky fellows when they left,' said Father Regan. 'They come back serious-minded, and what's more important, *spiritually-minded*. There is a new sincerity about them. If they're married outside the Church, they want to get things "fixed up." They want to "get the slate clean." Suffering does that to a man. It teaches him rock-bottom values, especially where his Faith is concerned.'

"There was a demonstration of that, that very afternoon. In one of the large quadrangles of the hospital, several hundred patients were being unloaded. One was a man who had been picked up on a raft after floating for days in the Pacific. He hadn't been removed from the ambulance before he was asking for a priest. 'I promised that if I came back alive, I'd get to Confession and Communion right off!' God had kept his end of the bargain; Bill was hurrying to do the same.

" 'Our Lady of Victory' . . . Victory over pain and fear and black discouragement. Victory that breeds confidence and high hope. Our Lady must love that chapel."

The afternoon I visited the chapel, I asked Father Regan who had done the murals. He said, "A young Jewish corpsman, in his spare time." The altar and many fixtures were made and donated enthusiastically by civilian workmen, Catholic and Protestant, and they had had their hearts in their work. As we left the chapel, there was a young sailor kneeling near the sanctuary. He had come to make his afternoon visit before the Blessed Sacrament.

"Men who were good Catholics before seeing action," Father Regan has said, "are grateful for their faith; quietly sure and calmly positive that their God was ever with them in their foxholes and that He saw them through. Men whose Faith may have slipped a little, were brought to abrupt consciousness of their need for prayer and spiritual aid 'out there.' "

CHAPTER XXI

The Captain Wears a Cross

ONE MORNING IN early June, 1942, when the battle of
Midway was hanging in the balance, Father Walter
Mahler and I, with orders to proceed to the mainland,
gathered our impedimenta and drove to the Merry Point
Landing at Pearl Harbor. That trip marked the end of
a four-year tour of duty of which two and a half years
were spent in Hawaiian waters. Wearing on my shoulder
marks the four stripes of a captain gave me the feeling
that my departure implied the end of my last sea cruise.
The seniority acquired after twenty-five years in the Navy,
sixteen of them spent at sea, rather precluded any chance
of being again assigned to duty on board a ship. It would
hardly do to have more rank than the skipper. The prospect of serving "on the beach" the remainder of my years
of active service with the colors saddened me a little. As I
stood on the landing, thoughts came to me about the life
I had led in our immaculately clean ships; the bugle calls
and the staccato orders on the morning of getting underway for a long cruise; the well ordered days at sea and
the evenings on deck at the movies under a full tropic
moon; voyages to foreign ports; an audience with the
Holy Father in Rome; the long cruises to Rio de Janiero
and to Santiago; living and working with Navy men
whom I came to know as friends for life; all this and more

passed before me in panorama as I stood that morning on the landing at Pearl Harbor.

I had learned that a Navy chaplain is free and unhampered in his religious work, and that a priest can become a strong influence in the life of non-Catholics. On board ship, the chaplain is the pastor of all hands, and a great part of his work has to do with men of other faiths. The key man in my work as entertainment officer on board the battleship *Mississippi* was my good friend Sam Soboloff, an orthodox Jew and, as the saying goes, a "great guy." Lee "Red" Durbin, the yeoman who served with me so faithfully and well in the Pacific Fleet, is a Methodist. My present yeoman, Lyle Johnson, a worthy successor to "Red," is a Presbyterian. Protestant men come to depend upon their priest shipmate and to trust in him with a faith equal to that of the Catholic men.

It is surprising how few people there are who know of the work of a Navy chaplain. Most priests entertain strange ideas about his job. Some may even dub it a sinecure. I wonder how many secular priests there are, after twenty-seven years in the priesthood, who find themselves still doing the work of junior curates, running sick-calls to the hospital ship, keeping office hours daily, having to ask permission to leave the ship, handling such collateral duties as librarian, athletic officer, editor of the ship's paper, mediator in family problems of the men, entertainment officer whose duty it is to manage movies, smokers, dances, sight-seeing parties, and the rest.

In answer to many letters which, a few years ago, I received from priests who were considering applying for a chaplaincy, I wrote an article for the *Ecclesiastical Review*. I said: "Many a good priest has failed to be a good chaplain through lack of aptitude or desire to live and to share with those to whom he was sent as a spiritual father. He should earnestly try to mix with his mess and shipmates on board and ashore. He has little excuse to be lonely. Although he is often separated from his fellow priests for weeks at a time, he soon feels quite at home in this strange world of ships and guns, for good company is plentiful wherever the Navy goes. You may be sure that he is able, through his prayers and his daily Mass, to retain the spirit of the good priest. He feels that Saints Peter, James and John are his constant support—for they too were sea-faring men. And St. Paul, his hero of ships and God, spoke the same language. His fellow officers and the men in the Fleet respect his mission, and they will take him to their hearts if he proves genuine.

"A Navy priest, as a career man, has little to look forward to if his life's work be judged according to the standard of his tradition and training as a secular. The purple is far over the horizon and practically unattainable. As a commissioned officer, his associates accept him or reject him for what he is rather than for the handsome uniform or the Roman collar he may wear. I consider this a hard test but a good one for any priest to meet. It is clear in the mind of the writer to-day that when he, some fifteen years ago vaguely questioned the wisdom of his decision to remain in the Navy, it was due to a desire for the sympathetic atmosphere of a Catholic neighborhood. For the chaplain, there is always the consoling conviction, should he ever feel discouraged, that he is giving more of himself to his apostolate than any secular priest of his acquaintance. The work is difficult, but the opportunities to serve God are boundless. What more could one want?

"He who marks the fitness reports of a Navy priest is not his bishop but his commanding officer. In view of the fact that the Navy Regulations require that a commanding officer report at least twice a year on an officer, covering specifically his qualifications as to intelligence, judgment, initiative, force, leadership, moral courage, co-operation, loyalty, perseverance, reactions in emergencies, endurance, industry, military bearing, and neatness of person and dress, it is evident that if a Chaplain is satisfactory in all these respects, he has certainly 'made the grade.' "

As fleet chaplain, my work was partially outlined in Navy Regulations, Section 1, Duties of the Fleet Chaplain, 1244:

"The duties of the Fleet Chaplain shall be as follows:

(a) To inspect the work of chaplains at frequent intervals.

(b) To advise, counsel, and offer suggestions to the Chaplains of the Fleet concerning their work.

(c) To arrange for services on board ships that do not carry chaplains; to arrange for interchange of chaplains of the different faiths so as to provide services for all.

(d) To call frequent meetings of chaplains of the Fleet for conference, discussion, and adjustment of the matters pertaining to their work.

(e) At the end of each quarter, he shall make a written report to the Chief of the Bureau of Navigation concerning the chaplains and their work."

My orders to the training station in San Diego meant that I would become the senior chaplain and, with the aid of two seasoned chaplains, conduct a course of indoctrination for a stream of newly commissioned churchmen standing by for orders to sea or to the Marine Corps.

In Hawaii, I was privileged to witness the drama of war from the prologue in 1939 to the murder scene in the second act on December seventh. I now was leaving that theatre with the hope that at a training station, I might help train a fighting cast for the victorious ending in the last act.

At the Pearl Harbor landing, the thoughtful John Kangeter greeted us from the stern sheets of a yard motor-boat. He had arranged for this special trip in his own efficient way and I thought it quite appropriate that my Aloha should be tied in with the Kangeter family for they symbolized for me the allurement of Hawaiian hospitality.

The boat took us across the bay to Ford Island where we found a ship which was taking on a cargo of planes in need of major repairs. Near the gangway, I found the skipper, my old friend, Captain Paul R. Glutting. The last time I saw Paul when he was on duty, was a Sunday morning in 1929 in Barcelona, Spain. He was then the gunnery officer of one of the battleships which took the regiment of midshipmen on a practice cruise to southern Europe. In mid-Atlantic, when we were making plans for a Mass in Barcelona, I recommended to the commander of the squadron, the late Rear Admiral Horace Laning, that Glutting be given command of the church party. Hundreds of officers, midshipmen and sailors came from the three ships, filling all the launches and motor-boats available and they marched down the boulevard behind an augmented band to attend a Solemn High Mass in the Church of St. Stephen.

Before the war she had been a "sea train" and was engaged in running loaded railway cars from New York to Havana, returning, I presume, with a cargo of Cuban products. The Navy found good use for her spacious compartments, stowing fighter planes there in great numbers and carrying them to the battle zones of the South Pacific.

She carried only four passengers on that June run to the mainland. Besides Father Mahler and myself, there were Ensigns Robert Nix, an artist, and Cole L. Windham, an aviator. We slept in a tiny room on cots that were wedged between a table and the bulkhead. The ship vibrated so strangely that it reminded me of my first ride on the back of a camel the day we officers of the destroyer *McCormick* inspected the Sphinx near Cairo.

On Sunday morning at sea, I celebrated an early Mass on topside and Father Mahler at ten o'clock conducted a general service for all hands and then offered Mass. My friend, whose record is outstanding in the corps, gave a good practical sermon which the crew thoroughly appreciated.

To this day, I am not certain about the nature of Bob Nix's war mission. He had served on board the *Yorktown* for many months, while attached to a torpedo squadron. It seemed his paramount job was to paint battle scenes for the official archives of the Navy. One night, he broke out a large roll of canvases and showed us the painting he made of the carrier *Lexington* just prior to the moment she went down. The colors in the painting were authentic, for Bob stood on the flight deck of the *Yorktown* and recorded in oils that heart-breaking scene.

The long and tedious passage to San Diego troubled Nix and Windham a bit more than it did us padres. Nix remarked one night in our stuffy cubicle, "The only exercise I get on this ship is jumping at conclusions." For myself, I welcomed the temporary escape it gave from the telephone, the U.S.O. meetings and countless interviews with homesick sailors. I read Robert Casey's "I Can't Forget."

On a damp and misty morning, the lumbering ship quietly slipped past Point Loma, rounded North Island and moored at the air station dock. We got our baggage on board a motor launch and crossed the bay to San Diego. Windham decided to leave at once for the east coast but I persuaded Father Mahler and Bob Nix to stay with me at my home in the foothills. On the dock at the foot of Broadway, I telephoned the tenant who had occupied Casa de Anita for over two years and learned that we could at once take possession.

My orders read that I should first report to the commandant of the 11th Naval District, Rear Admiral Ralston Holmes, with whom twenty years before I had served on board the *Idaho*. We had a pleasant chat in his office.

From there I went to the chancery office and paid my respects to the Most Reverend Charles F. Buddy, Bishop of San Diego and a Vicar Delegate of the armed forces. The Bishop, as always, was most cordial and deeply interested in my work.

I next made a hurried call on the District Chaplain, Harrill S. Dyer, with whom I had served on my last tour of shore duty. He was carrying a heavy burden involving Navy relief, housing, and the task of consoling and advising the widows of those lost in battle. Harrill, in his philosophic way, was taking it in stride. He was still a big league pitcher. Although his contract signed years ago with the Cleveland Indians had expired, he was "in there with lots of stuff on the ball."

It felt good to be home again. Sprawling on a knoll which gave a view of the Pacific, the white hacienda with its red tiled roof and Navy blue windows had the charm of a dream made real. The first thing that caught my eye was what had once been a dwarf fir tree which an enterprising Jap gardener had sold me for a pretty sum. In four years, it had become the tallest tree in the rock garden. A Jap joke, perhaps. Bushes and vines were in bloom and the roses were all smiles.

We set up bachelor hall. Bob Nix volunteered to cook with the definite proviso that he would have nothing to do with the dishes. He expertly won our hearts by a deft juggling of Louisiana recipes, especially salads, which only an artist should ever strive to achieve. But Father Mahler and I, although we gained skill as mess cooks and never dropped a wet dish, frequently had unsuspecting help, for we often invited Father Tommy Regan to dine —and to join us afterward in the kitchen while the obstinate Bob Nix sat alone in the living-room reading the funnies.

My first public appearance after arriving home was in the little Church of St. Martin, in La Mesa. Father Thomas Lehane, the pastor, invited me to celebrate Mass and to preach. My old friend and neighbor, Lieutenant Commander Thomas Hayes, and his family were there. John, their son, who once managed my lime grove, had just joined the Marine Corps as a paratrooper, and Mary, the eldest daughter, already had thoughts of becoming a WAAC. The congregation seemed interested in what I had to say about the war. Tom Hayes later said he liked my saying, "This is not a singing war; it is a fighting war." I may have had in mind the contrast so apparent between Hawaii and its martial law, black-out and scarcity of food and the untroubled life in Southern California. This was in the days before rationing when a man thought he was a patriot if he displayed little American flags on the fenders of his car even though he "burned up the highway" wasting gas and rubber at seventy miles an hour. It looked as though it would take more than Pearl Harbor to convince the people of the mainland that a grim war for existence was underway.

When my late sister's children returned from boarding school, life in Casa de Anita acquired a quicker tempo. Their home stands on a neighboring hill. Jack Nolan, the eldest boy, often came to the house although he had begun a course of study which he hoped might some day lead to a commission in the Marine Corps. Roger Michael, a twelve-year-old first lieutenant and his brother Bill, a ten-year-old sergeant, arrived from St. Catherine's Military School at Anaheim, California. It interested me to learn how capably the Dominican Nuns conducted a military school for boys. I had attended the graduation exercises and admired the soldierly qualities of the young cadets. My niece, Anita "Baba" Nolan, was on vacation from the Flintridge Sacred Heart Academy, at Pasadena. Soon after she arrived during a ten days leave, we motored to Los Angeles to buy a dog. We visited a likely looking kennel where the owner showed us a litter of Cocker spaniel puppies. All were jet black but one little fellow who had a buff colored coat. We immediately decided to take him with us and we called him Buffer, for he gave promise of being a real buffer between the worries of the market place and the serenity of a home on a hill.

Bob Nix stayed with us during most of my days of leave. One afternoon when we thought it about time that Nix broke out the galley gear and got the evening chow on the fire, he could not be found. After a brief search, we went to his room where we found him half kneeling on a chair, painting. In his left hand he held a cluster of Cherokee roses which he was rapidly painting in water colors. Sensing our presence, he grunted, "Just like me to choose a white rose—the hardest thing in the world to paint." It is a beautiful piece of work and it hangs today with other treasures of my Navy career near the fireplace in my home.

CHAPTER XXII

Dependables

WHEN I CALLED at the office of the commandant of the 11th Naval District, Rear Admiral Ralston S. Holmes, our conversation naturally veered to the days in 1919 when we were shipmates in the *Idaho*. The Admiral, who then had the rank of commander, was the executive officer and our duties on board brought us in daily contact. The *Idaho* had a crew of fourteen hundred men and not all of them were enjoying freedom from personal troubles.

Our commanding officer was the late Rear Admiral Carl T. Vogelgesang, a distinguished officer, and one of the strongest and noblest characters I have ever known. He was then a captain in his last ship command and he instilled in us some of his own spirit. We helped him make the *Idaho* one of the smartest ships in the Fleet.

In personal matters, I seldom went to the captain. The "exec," who is second in command, is the one to whom the chaplain goes to help solve the problems of the crew. One morning, with strong misgivings, I went to Commander Holmes' cabin with what seemed an impossible request. Tony Lancia, a seaman, had asked me to help him get a transfer from the Pacific Fleet which was then based at San Pedro, California, to the European station. He had received a letter from relatives in Italy telling him that his brother, an Italian soldier, lay in danger of

145

death in a hospital in Milan. Every chaplain knows it is difficult enough to have a man transferred to another ship in the same fleet let alone to a naval squadron six thousand miles away. But Commander Holmes found a way. There was a supply ship alongside the *Idaho* that morning and she was scheduled to sail for the east coast. Holmes also knew that the destroyer division 39 was fitting out in the Philadelphia yard for duty in Turkish waters. That day, Tony Lancia with bag and hammock, and a broad grin on his weather-beaten face, climbed on board the supply ship and headed toward the Panama Canal.

The executive officer remembered Tony Lancia and how he made good on board the *Idaho* "in the hard way." One afternoon, following a period of strenuous drill in number two turret, Tony, who then was rather small, weighing about 135 pounds, came to my room and showed me a discolored eye that would have challenged the skill of the Brooklyn artists on Sands Street who make a living "painting out black eyes." Tony was in a rage.

"What happened, shipmate?" I asked him.

"MacDonald socked me, Sir." He referred to the leading bosun's mate of the division. "I was mindin' my own business, Father, and he up and socks me in the eye."

I offered the lad a chair and a cigarette and assured him that no petty officer on board had the right to "sock" a seaman. After restoring Tony to a degree of calm, I sent him to sick bay where a hospital corpsman painted over his eye a round moon of iodine the size of a sauce-pan. The next day, the brown spot had lost none of its striking appeal when Tony and MacDonald appeared on the quarterdeck at the captain's mast.

MacDonald was on the report for striking Tony Lancia.

Captain Vogelgesang spoke first to the plantiff. "Lancia, what have you to say?"

"Sir," replied Tony, "MacDonald socked me in the eye."

The Captain turned to the big Irishman. "What have you to say, MacDonald? I trust you know that Navy regulations forbid this sort of thing?"

"Well, Sir," replied the bosun's mate, "I think I've got the best division on the ship. I want to put an 'E' on our turret, but Lancia here has been gold brickin'. He ain't puttin' out. He's the slowest guy in the division. I warned him but it didn't do any good. So I tapped him on the eye to snap him out of it."

The Captain struggled to suppress a smile. "Lancia, the second division is one of the best in the ship. Evidently you've been lagging behind. I want you to prove you are as good as the best. MacDonald, knock off tapping your men. Lancia, go forward and show me you're a good man-o-war's man."

Three years later when I became the chaplain of the Navy destroyer squadron serving in Turkish waters, I went ashore in Constantinople. As I rode in an arabah on the Pera, I saw, standing in front of the Y.M.C.A., my old shipmate, Tony Lancia. I told the Turk to stop and I greeted Tony. He told me that a month after he left the *Idaho*, he arrived in Philadelphia in time to manage a transfer to the destroyer *Litchfield* which had sailing orders to Europe. When the 39th Division reached Naples where it remained for a week, Tony requested leave and went to Milan to visit his soldier brother in the hospital. I thought, when Tony told me about it, of the kindness of Commander Ralston Holmes.

One night, when I stood on the navigating bridge of

the *Litchfield* on a cruise in the eastern Mediterranean, I noticed standing in the dark with his hands gripping the wheel, my friend Lancia. That night I thought of Mac-Donald, the bosun's mate, and the day he made a man-o-war's man of a young sailor by "socking" him in the eye.

Ten years after Lancia left the *Idaho* to visit his brother in Italy, I sat in my room on board the *Black Hawk* at Chefoo, North China. Someone tapped on the door and I said, "Come in." To my happy surprise, it was Tony, now a rugged, barrel-chested bosun's mate first class. His destroyer was alongside the tender for repairs and Tony came over for a chat about old times. He was a true man-o-war's man and extremely proud of his profession. He had become eminently dependable.

One evening in the Coronado home of my old friends, the Walter Fitches, they told a story of a Marine who proved his dependability in a rather spectacular fashion. The lad was the orderly of Walter's cousin, Rear Admiral Aubrey Fitch, whose flagship, the *Lexington*, was lost in battle in the Solomons. The Admiral and his orderly stood on deck waiting for the ship's company to abandon ship when the young Marine, with a large bundle under his arm, said, "Admiral, pardon me, Sir, but don't you think it's time for you to leave? The ship's sinkin', Sir."

The Admiral turned to his orderly and replied, "Son, I will be the last to leave. Go and get into a boat."

With his heavy bundle, the orderly managed somehow to lower himself over the side on a manila line and to climb aboard a motor launch. The Admiral soon followed him. Lowering himself hand-over-hand down the hull of the big "flat-top," he got to within twenty feet of the water when the skin of his hands became so badly burned he had to let go. It was quite a drop but he landed unhurt in a motor launch which, by pure chance, was under him. When the Admiral recovered from the effects of the fall, he noticed a Marine standing before him. It was his orderly holding the contents of the bundle. "Here's your overcoat, Admiral. I thought you'd be needin' it."

On his way to join the Asiatic Fleet in the summer of 1941, Chaplain Father McGarrity of Philadelphia, enjoyed a short stopover in Honolulu. The evening of the day he arrived, he came to the Pacific Club for dinner and he convinced me very quickly that the Navy had added to the chaplain corps a man of exceptional ability and personal charm. Although he knew that he was stepping into the lion's den, his sole thought was to reach the "Asiatics" and report aboard the old carrier *Langley* and get to work. He seemed interested when I told him that I had served in the middle twenties as the carrier's first chaplain. I told him how good the pilots had to be in those days to land their "crates" on the old "Covered Wagon" when she was making her top speed of eleven knots. I did not know then that Father McGarrity was to be the *Langley's* last chaplain, that he would be aboard her when the fine old ship went down in battle in the Java Sea. It is reported that the oil tanker *Pecos* rescued the *Langley's* survivors only to be sunk the following day by Jap dive-bombers. The handsome young padre is listed as "missing in action." May God protect him.

Whenever I recall the days I spent in our first plane carrier when it was new and thrilling to stand in the nets that hung below the level of the flight deck and see our pioneer carrier pilots take off and land, not always successfully, I think of Captain Stanford Moses who then commanded the air squadrons. He was not a pilot and, for that reason, his task was more difficult than the aviators who later assumed his responsibilities.

Captain Moses was a member of a distinguished Jewish family of the South. He was more the scholarly executive than a rugged, war-time man of action. He was medium height, slender and strikingly good looking and his voice was modulated so that you felt he would be kind with a sailor when caught on the rocks and shoals of life.

I enjoyed our talks in his cabin especially when he outlined his thoughts regarding the sailor's uniform. Captain Moses advocated discarding the sailor's jumper and bell-bottomed trousers with the thirteen buttons and giving him, instead, a jacket with double-breasted buttons. He argued, with good reason, that the ancient uniform of the bluejacket which gives him little pocket room for the things he needs on liberty, was not any longer practical; he thought a more dapper costume would also increase a sailor's self-respect. He admired the uniform of the Marine and he felt that the similarity between the buck private's uniform and that of his regimental commander had a lot to do in fostering the "leatherneck's" esprit de corps.

The "Commodore," as we called the commander of the aircraft squadrons, held the American man-o-war's man in high esteem as the most versatile, loyal and dependable man in the world. His stories were mostly about the sailors he had commanded at sea, how the young recruit changed for the better when he responded to the training and the strict life the Navy demands of the sailor.

One evening in the cabin of the *Langley*, Captain Moses told of an experience he once had in San Francisco when his command, the battleship *Arkansas*, was visiting that popular rendezvous of the fleet. As was customary, the skipper went ashore one afternoon in civilian clothes and, while strolling up Market Street, he noticed a crowd of idlers milling about on the sidewalk. His curiosity aroused, he elbowed his way to the center of the group where he found a man lying unconscious. Before he had a chance to do anything for the sick man, a lad brushed him aside and yelled, "Give the guy air." He then took off his coat and handed it to the Captain, ordering him to " 'phone for the ambulance and chop, chop." Then again to the bystanders, "And you birds, stand back and give the guy some air." When the Captain returned from the telephone booth, the good samaritan was on his knees giving the sick man artificial respiration.

By the time the ambulance arrived, he had his patient sitting up and breathing normally. The bystanders slowly walked away. Captain Moses, handing the man his coat, said, "Fine work, young man; where did you learn all this? Are you a medical student?"

"No," was the reply, "I used to be in the Navy. They taught me first aid. That job was right up my alley."

The Captain was impressed. "I'm proud of you, son. I'm in the Navy myself." He then told the lad his name.

"Holy smoke! I'm sorry, Sir, for ordering you around like that. How was I to know?"

That evening Captain Moses and the ex-bluejacket had dinner together, and the check was "on the Old Man."

A sailor's dependability and all-around usefulness was literally built into my home. One day the builder came to me and said, "Perhaps you would like to know that one of my carpenters is an ex-bluejacket. He came to me looking for a job, and his only recommendation was an honorable discharge from the Navy and the rating of carpenter's mate, first class. I told the lad I had no doubt he could repair boats but I questioned his ability to build a house. He pleaded for a try-out and I took him on. In the past two months I have raised his pay three times. He is the cleverest and most dependable man in my outfit. The Navy does something to a man."

CHAPTER XXIII

Boot Camp

ON THE SHORE of San Diego Bay lies the most attractive of all our naval training stations. The buildings are appropriately of Spanish design, in beige stucco, and the roofs are of red tile. The lawns and trees are so carefully tended that you feel when you enter the main gate you are approaching a well-kept university campus. For twenty years, young men from the southern and western states have come here for fundamental lessons in how to serve in the fleet in the honored uniform of a man-o-war's man.

Five years before the outbreak of World War II, I reported for duty at the training station and remained for two years, when I was ordered to duty in the fleet. There were only two chaplains assigned there in those days. During the first year, Chaplain Harrill S. Dyer was my Protestant colleague. Chaplain Razzie W. Truitt relieved him in the summer of 1937. We could not have chosen a more enjoyable peace-time assignment. The number of recruits never exceeded four thousand and this enabled us to know them more intimately than it is possible to know them today.

When I reported in the summer of 1942, the station had expanded to such an extent that ten chaplains were on duty there looking after the spiritual needs of the

thousands of young recruits who had joined up to fight
the global war. There were thirty-five thousand men under
training, distributed among the recruit camps and the
many schools which are run to fit men for the more difficult jobs the modern warship requires of her personnel.
But nothing was sacrificed with respect to the attractive-
ness of the station. The new buildings had the character
of permanency and the landscaping was carefully planned
so that you felt the station had always been the size of
a city.

The days immediately following the Pearl Harbor raid
witnessed an avalanche of recruits surging through the
gates and it called for night and day hard labor on the
part of the commanding officer and his staff. To Captain
Henry C. Gearing, U.S.N., great credit is due for the
successful handling of the emergency. In rapid succession,
new buildings for offices, barracks, libraries, auditoriums
and shops sprang up and covered a vast area reaching
beyond the dreams of anyone not aware of the demands of
total war. When I reported, most of the new buildings
were being occupied. Only the three large recreation cen-
ters were still unfinished and the North and South Chapels
were in blueprints. Our chapels were completed in the
fall under the close supervision of Captain Gearing and
the chaplains.

The senior Protestant chaplain was Captain Ernest
L. Ackiss, an old friend whom I had known since the First
World War. In 1940, Ackiss relieved me as scouting force
chaplain in Hawaii. He was known in the fleet for his
energy and excellent judgment and I was glad we were
to be so closely associated in our daily work. Before the
chaplain's division expanded with the others, Ackiss had
two experienced assistants, Chaplain Everett P. Wueb-

bens, a Lutheran, and Father Francis A. Burke. In the spring of 1942, many newly commissioned chaplains reported fresh from civil life. They came before the opening of the chaplains' school at Norfolk, Virginia, and were, in a sense, recruits, and also faced a problem of adjustment. But it took only a few weeks for them to understand the organization of the training station and to learn how their work might help in the making of the man-o-war's man.

"The mission of the Training Department," as one reads in the Station Regulations, "is to bridge the gap for the recruits from civilian to military life, introducing and instilling within them naval discipline and fundamental duties.

"Special emphasis is placed on the above in view of the fact that the majority of recruits received are at an age where character may be molded. The inculcating of an intelligent conception of discipline, and the transforming of the recruit from an immature boy to a self-reliant disciplined man-of-war's man is the prime requisite of this department, and this fact shall be borne in mind by all officers and company commanders.

"In order to accomplish this mission, the fundamental subjects which shall comprise the curriculum of training are: small boats, swimming, infantry and extended drill pertaining to landing force operations, classifications for future training, small arms, gas warfare defense, seamanship, ordnance, and taking care of themselves."

The recruits come by train and bus from points west of the Mississippi and south as far as the Gulf and the Mexican border. They arrive at any time of the day or night, presenting a composite portrait of high-school youth, looking and acting, when you first see them, as though they just had stepped down from a well-inscribed "jalopy." Their sports clothes and small-town hair cuts and studied carelessness fairly conceal a state of genuine bewilderment which surely has them in its grip. No time is lost in literally getting down to the bare truth, for after the barbers have shorn his locks, the Navy doctors and dentists quickly place the embryo sailor under careful examination. They give vaccinations, blood tests, x-rays of chest and typhoid inoculations. If the recruit arrives in the morning, he draws his Navy outfit in the afternoon and begins marking his clothing. He draws his marked bedding, marches to chow and then prepares to turn in at the sound of taps, and that solemn call seems to say, "And I do mean you."

"Rise and shine!" greets the young recruit at 5:30 the next morning. He is still one of the undisciplined herd and he wonders what it is all about. There remains the job of marking and rolling clothes, removing tags and lacing gussets. On the third day, much to his relief, he joins a company made up of one hundred and sixty men. He meets his company commander and if he has made a good impression, he probably discovers that he has been appointed a recruit petty officer. Previous experience at a military school usually wins a man a position of leadership in his company. On the fourth day, the recruit draws a rifle and bayonet and undertakes to master the Manual of Arms. He attends lecture A on "Discipline and Duty" and lecture B on "What the Service Offers." He scrubs his clothes and then goes to his first Navy movie.

On the fifth day, he probably wonders whether he is really in the Navy for he is still drilling like an infantry man.

Several years ago at the Newport training station, a

new recruit became so exasperated with daily marching on the "grinder" that he stepped out of ranks, walked over to his company commander and cried, "I joined the Navy to go to sea. I don't want to be a soldier. I'm through." He then grabbed the barrel of his rifle, swung the gun over his head and smashed the butt into splinters on the hard pavement. Suddenly realizing what he had done, he ran like a rabbit across the drill grounds intending to "go over the hill" and catch the first bus for home. But he ran in the wrong direction and came to a dead stop on the north shore of the island. After three days on a diet of bread and water in the station brig, the young apprentice seaman came to his senses.

In every capital ship there is a landing force made up of bluejackets and they are smart infantry men. When they assemble with packs and rifles on the quarterdeck, they perhaps recall that on their fifth day in the Navy they learned how to clean their rifles and scrub their leggings. They may also remember that they attended lecture C on "Enlistment, Discharges and Courts Martial" and that on that day they were introduced to the book called "Navy Regulations."

On the sixth day, the captain holds inspection and casts a seaman's eye upon his neophytes as they march past in a free, sailor-like swing. He is pleased, for he knows that the recruit has passed the first milestone and now has behind him the countless annoyances that bedevil the Navy "boot."

Then comes the Lord's day when the Navy hoists the Church pennant above the Stars and Stripes and orders all men in training to assemble at Divine Worship. From 6:30 A.M. until 10.15 A.M., the chaplains hold twenty services in chapels and auditoriums for Protestants, Jews and Catholics. Special meetings are also held on Sundays and other days for Christian Scientists and Mormons.

There are two all-purpose chapels on the station which are so designed as to be adaptable to the needs of the three recognized religious groups, Protestants, Jews and Catholics. Each chapel, which holds about five hundred, has a wing which is used as a Catholic oratory and there the Blessed Sacrament is reserved. On week days, the priests offer evening Mass. On Sundays and week day mornings when more space is required, Masses are celebrated in the large Catholic chapel in one of the centrally located camps.

Rather than take the Catholic raw recruits to an auditorium for Sunday Mass, I conceived the idea of marching them, from spring to fall, under the clear California sky to the boxing arena which holds six thousand men. The main purpose is to remind them from the outset that they will seldom again attend Holy Mass in the quiet glow of stained glass windows or enjoy the richness of marble altars and Communion rails. It may help them to be reminded that even a boxing arena, a quarterdeck of a battleship, or the mess compartment of a cruiser can be quickly changed into a temple of worship. I have said something like this to the "boots." "Men, yesterday you were here with your eyes trained on this boxing ring. You saw your shipmates wage friendly battle with padded gloves. Today you see an altar where Holy Mass will be offered, the same Mass you have participated in back in the home-town church. From now on you will attend Mass in strange places, for the priest will be with you wherever you go. It's the Mass that matters and not the artistic trimmings. Therefore, let us place ourselves in the presence of God and humbly adore Him. . . . ." They sing their favorite hymns; they read aloud parts of the Mass, and in large numbers they come to the ring ropes to receive Our Savior in Holy Communion.

Perhaps the favorite chapel is the one dedicated to "Mary, Star of the Sea." It is in the wing of the North Chapel and it is really a thing of beauty. Although the commanding officer is not a Catholic, he took especial interest in obtaining everything that was required to make it a chapel worthy of a Catholic sailor's pride. In the corner of the sanctuary stands a statuette of "Mary, Star of the Sea." It is the work of a Carmelite nun of the San Diego monastery. The Reverend Mother Emmanuel, the Mother Superior, and a great friend of the Navy, presented it when the chapel was first built. The beautiful Stations of the Cross are a gift of a friend of the Navy, a New Yorker. The panels of the triptych above the altar were painted by two sailors who are on duty at the station. Many sailors and WAVES come during the day to make a visit before the tabernacle and, at four-thirty on weekday afternoons, the faithful come to assist at evening Mass.

After a week in the detention camp the recruits are fairly well "shaken down." They have met the chaplain, who, they discover, is their mentor and friend. His job is to help them over the rough spots on their journey to the fleet. The chaplains interview all the recruits and find out how they stand with respect to their religious needs. Many recruits come to have their marriages validated; others to be instructed for Confirmation, and still others to receive the very fundamentals in religious instruction.

A great deal of the chaplain's time in the "boot camp" is given to the homesick sailor. The small-town boy who, for the first time, has seen a crowd of over two hundred people, naturally feels uneasy in a regimented group of thousands of spirited youth and he yearns for the peace and independence of his front stoop.

I once heard Chaplain Harrill Dyer tell the recruits at San Diego, "Before you joined the Navy, you were told to do a job, but this is the first time that the fellow who tells you sticks around to see that you do it." He knew that he was addressing immature, happy-go-lucky American kids who found it tough going to take orders and promptly respond with a cheerful, "Aye, aye, Sir."

There are many recruits who enlisted without realizing the importance of a contract with the Government to serve for a period of years. Some will tearfully complain, "I didn't know it was like this—I want to go home," just as though they were freshmen in a boarding school. With patience and tact, the chaplain leads the youngster back on a true course and incidentally makes life much more pleasant for the regimental commander who probably wonders what the chaplain does "the other six days."

It is unfortunate, particularly in war time, that the relatives of our enlisted men have so little understanding of the responsibilities of a recruit. Their letters in many cases are the chief cause of a man's discouragement. They tell of the petty troubles in the home, or of illness, that has probably disappeared by the time the letter arrives, to harrow the sailor's soul. And they sound the gloomy call, "Come home."

I read lately a typical letter which a bluejacket showed me as his reason for requesting an "emergency leave" and a loan from the American Red Cross to finance a round-trip to Chicago. His Aunt Molly had written that her son Peter was in the hospital recovering from an operation. She wrote, "Please come home at once. It would do Peter good to see you." When I asked the recruit what he would do in the same circumstances if he were working for the Standard Oil Company, he suddenly saw how ridiculous the whole thing was.

Where thousands of men are gathered in one spot, it is to be expected that many emergency leaves are granted to visit a member of the immediate family who may be in danger of death. The message is first taken to the chaplain's office where there is always a chaplain on duty. The recruit is then sent for. The case is immediately investigated by the Red Cross and, if necessary, a loan is made and the man sent on his way.

Before the Navy expanded to its present size, the chaplains had more to do with the "machinery" of welfare work. When I reported in 1942, Chaplain Ackiss was editor of the weekly paper, *The Hoist*, which I had edited five years before. He also was officer in charge of insurance and supervised the work of thirty-five yeomen. I was soon placed in charge of the station libraries and held that job for many months until the Bureau of Naval Personnel placed all libraries under the judisdiction of the head of the Welfare Department. The Office of Public Relations took over *The Hoist*, and the business of selling Government insurance to the recruits and of assisting them in making out family allowances was turned over to the Training Department. This was probably a step in the right direction for it gave the chaplain a chance to devote his whole time to the needs of the individual recruit with complete freedom from the "indirect appeal."

As an old hand in welfare activities, it delighted me to find my friend Lieutenant George O'Brien, the movie star, as head man of the department of welfare and athletics. Coming from Hollywood where, for years, he wore the laurels of high achievement, George quickly proved that he was a naval officer at heart. When I arrived, he and his well-trained outfit were going full speed ahead on a welfare program that was amazing in that it benefited everyone. On a Saturday or Sunday afternoon, a tour of the station gave you a picture of sports activity that comprised mass boxing, softball, tennis, basket ball, football, and inter-company boxing-matches in the arena. His department also booked shows in which top-flight entertainers took part. But the dynamic personality of the popular George O'Brien was probably the chief factor in building a high state of morale among the recruits. His sincerity of purpose was apparent and the example he set of being at all times a model officer and shipmate was an influence for the young bluejackets which they will never forget.

When Henry Fonda, the movie star, became an apprentice seaman, George O'Brien and I thought we might haze him a bit. I had met Fonda at John Ford's home and liked him from the start. George, of course, had known Henry for years. One afternoon, we sent for him. I was prepared to greet him with something like this: "Good afternoon, son. Your name is Bonda, I believe." He must have been tipped off by my yeoman, Lyle Johnson, because he burst into my private office like a young colt, stood at attention and smartly said, "Good afternoon, Father. I'm glad you sent for me." We had a good laugh over it. Fonda was the most enthusiastic recruit on the station and he said that it had been pretty rough sledding the first few days in boot camp but he liked it. His only regret was that they had made him a recruit petty officer and that his additional duties hindered him from buying chocolate bars at the ship's service store. He said, "I'd give my right arm for a chocolate bar." Johnson reached into the drawer of his desk and saved the day.

Over half of the men who come to the training station, at the end of eight weeks of indoctrination, enter the many schools which the Navy conducts to train radio operators, quartermasters, aviation machinist mates, fire control men, and a dozen other ratings. Many men are sent also to various universities for special courses and again they head toward the coast, this time to take their places in ships of the battle line. After victory is won, they will return to their home towns, smarter and more dependable than they were the day they got their first "shots" at the Receiving Unit. They will have the Navy in their blood and they will show their pride one day when they break out the "memory book" and tell their children all about it.

CHAPTER XXIV

Barnstorming

IT MAY HAVE BEEN "Rig for Church" or the broadcast
"Report to Mothers and Fathers" which I gave on the
Catholic Hour from Honolulu that prompted so many to
invite me to speak during the twelve months that followed
my return to California. It was not easy to arrange to be
absent from the training station, nor was it necessary to
be reminded that my paramount duty as senior chaplain
was no sinecure. But I was conscious of having important
things to say to civilian workers and I was quite willing
that the Office of Public Relations arrange for speaking
engagements on the radio and at war plants in California.

While still on leave a few days after my arrival in San
Diego, I motored to Los Angeles to take part in the ceremony of presenting the Army and Navy "E" to the workers of the Consolidated Steel Corporation. A former shipmate of the China station days, Captain Gaylord Church,
was the naval inspector at the plant; he and his assistant,
Lieutenant Edward Sherry, whom I had known in Brest,
France, were evidently responsible for my being on the
program. When I addressed the crowd of three thousand
men and women who stood under a blazing sun, I felt that
I was voicing the feelings of my former shipmates in the
fleet when I praised them for their excellent performance
of duty. Father Tom Regan went with me on that trip and
he shared my distress when a traffic jam in Los Angeles

and a very long freight train delayed our arrival on the platform until a minute before the ceremony began. Punctuality is one of the virtues the Navy gives you; it is like committing a crime to be late.

A few weeks later, I was invited to "go on the air" with Nelson Eddy in Hollywood. It was a coast-to-coast broadcast in the interest of a popular cigarette and was intended to increase our war spirit. I took part in a dialogue with the eminent baritone and told briefly of the heroism of our men at Pearl Harbor. The studio was really a theatre where hundreds came, including my niece, Anita Nolan, to see and hear the goings on. It was a trying ordeal but I believe I was more tired than nervous. My friend, Commander A. Jack Bolton, the Public Relations officer, had met Anita and me at the train and first took us to his office where we saw him swear in a member of his office force as an ensign, and then to lunch at the Twentieth Century Fox Studio where Mary, the wife of John Ford, and their daughter Barbara joined us. We then went to a movie set where Henry Fonda was playing the leading role in a western. I did not realize then that Fonda, a few months later, would come to my office as a newly rated quartermaster, third class, to say good-by, glowing with enthusiasm over his orders to a fighting ship of the Pacific Fleet.

The Office of Public Relations in Los Angeles asked me in September to take part in a radio dramatization of a few exciting incidents of my Navy life. It was then a custom, and for all I know it still is, to have the studio actors enact a scene or two and then to introduce "in the voice," as it were, the real person. The broadcast was given in the National Broadcasting studio in Hollywood. I took my niece Anita along for she found that sort of activity amusing. She enjoyed meeting celebrities, and it delighted me to have her moral support in that tiresome business. After the Navy broadcast late in the afternoon, the producer of the drama introduced us to Kay Kyser who was about to give his hour of fun called the Kollege of Musical Knowledge. He invited us to attend the show and gave us seats in the front row of the large auditorium. Before the show began, the comedian, in pea-green cap and gown, invited my sixteen-year-old companion to assist him on the stage in lining up the contestants for "Kollege" honors. Anita found it great fun and so did I, until, in the middle of the program, Kyser made a speech. He said, "Students, we have in the studio tonight, Father Maguire, the chaplain who was at Pearl Harbor on December seventh. He left his altar, grabbed a gun, and fired at the Japs, yelling, 'Praise the Lord and pass the ammunition.' " The "mike" was too far away for me to nip in the bud a story which went merrily around the world. The next day, the *Los Angeles Times* ran a story with the caption, "Chaplain-Gunner Tells of Pearl Harbor Attack." I believe journalists call this peculiar type of reporting "ballyhoo." The *Times* reporter had by-passed Jack Bolton's Office of Public Relations and started the ball rolling from coast to coast and wrapped around the "ball" was a song which memorialized a Navy chaplain who was called, "A son of a gun of a gunner."

Returning to the training station, I showed the *Times* story to the commanding officer, Captain H. C. Gearing, and wrote out an official statement denying I had fired a gun at Pearl Harbor. Aside from the falsity of the report, I resented being accused of violating the Geneva Convention which had placed chaplains in the category of non-combatants. I called on Rear Admiral Ralston S.

Holmes and gave him an account of the ridiculous shenanigan. But the story helped to "plug" a war song which attained the uncertain honor of being on the radio "Hit Parade."

The radio program called "The March of Time" accepted the song's lyric as based on fact and I again went over the ether waves as a shouting gunner-parson and the author of the war's best slogan. That might have been the end of it had I not been ordered one day to fly to Washington for temporary duty in connection with the selection of officers for promotion in the chaplain corps. One afternoon, the day I left for San Diego, I was in the office of Captain Robert D. Workman, Chief of Chaplains, when the Director of Public Relations, Captain Leland P. Lovett, inquired whether I would care to make the principal Navy Day address in Detroit. I assured him I was quite willing if the Navy felt I could fill the bill. A few days after I reached San Diego, orders arrived, but in the same mail, clippings from Detroit papers came telling about the "Chaplain-Gunner" who was to speak on October 27th. I wired the Navy Day Committee to set them straight for the sake of the truth.

Leaving Los Angeles at noon on the "Chief," I went early to the diner and found I was the only customer there but I was by no means neglected for suddenly I heard, coming from the pantry, soft tones of a good quartette rendering "Praise the Lord and Pass the Ammunition." I paid for that brief concert with many autographs all the way to Chicago.

The Navy Day Committee which included Harvey Campbell of the Detroit Board of Commerce, George M. Slocum, the publisher, Monsignor Edward Hickey, Chancellor of the Archdiocese of Detroit, and many other hospitable citizens, honored me with a three-day routine that would have amazed a member of the President's cabinet.

At seven on a cold October morning, Patrick Shea and a companion met me at the railway station and took me to the Book-Cadillac Hotel where we had breakfast. The newspaper boys and girls came at ten for an interview. They promised to soft-peddle the imaginary gun play at Pearl Harbor and they were true to their word. They took pictures. Shortly after they left, I was told that the late Edsel Ford had invited the Navy Day Committee and me to have lunch with him at the plant. When we arrived, it was announced that our host, at the last moment, had been detained. Mr. Sorenson presided. In addition to several executives of the Ford "empire" whom I met at luncheon was Earl Godwin, the radio commentator. He asked a question at the table which made me feel as though he had placed a hot potato in my hand. He wanted to know whether I thought a boy of eighteen was too young to be inducted into the armed forces. It was at the time when Congress was debating the question, and I was not a bit anxious to be quoted on the air. I reminded Godwin that being a Navy man, my opinion had to do only with the bluejacket and that I thought there were many ratings in the Navy which an eighteen-year-old boy could hold capably. A young teen-age fellow then took pictures.

That afternoon, we inspected the Willow Run bomber plant which proved what great war strides Ford had made in less than a year. Someone said the roof of the plant was large enough to cover eleven football fields. On our way back to the hotel, we stopped at a huge building where I met several executives of General Motors Company who showed me, among many other war devices, an anti-aircraft gun of a new type they were turning out for the fleet. Again a cameraman got busy. This new role of being a guest of a high-pressure city like Detroit fairly spun my head like a top.

After dining that evening with the committee's chairman, George M. Slocum, and his wife, I motored to Windsor, Canada, and called on the American vice consul, Charles C. Sundell. I had married "Sunny" and Gertrud in Chefoo, North China, in 1931 when he was the vice consul at that summer base of the destroyer squadron. I enjoyed a pleasant chat with the Sundells about those happier days when we had many mutual friends on the China station.

When I returned to the hotel that evening, I discovered that the Navy Day Committee had moved my bags to a larger suite and I was glad to hear that Lanny Ross, the star of radio and screen, was to occupy one of the rooms. He was in Detroit to take part in an opera and planned to leave by plane, immediately after the performance, for New York. When he was told about Navy Day, he generously offered to postpone his departure and to lend a hand on the program.

At eleven in the morning, I was taken to Cadillac Square where I addressed a hundred or more Navy recruits who had come to be inducted into the Navy. With them were hundreds of their friends and they seemed especially pleased when the popular Lanny Ross sang the national anthem. From there we went to the City Hall where, at 11:45, I met Mayor Edward J. Jeffries who, a few months later, addressed a large gathering and introduced me from the City Hall steps as "the Chaplain who fired the gun at Pearl Harbor." He hadn't got the word. Having jumped over that hurdle, I carried on with a brief "pep talk" to the multitude. Promptly at 12:05 P.M., the party proceeded to the Founder's Room in the Book-Cadillac Hotel where, at a sort of reception, I met Mrs. Edwin H. Denby, the widow of the former Secretary of the Navy, and the Honorable Truman Newberry who also held that post in the cabinet.

The banquet hall held at least two thousand people among whom were women members of twenty patriotic organizations. I was a bit awe-struck but I pretended to be unmoved by the scene and the prospect of addressing an audience which the year before had heard the Honorable Frank Knox, Secretary of the Navy, as principal speaker on Navy Day.

Following a short speech by Mayor Jeffries, the Reverend Frank Fitt, Pastor of Grosse Point Memorial Church, introduced me. He spoke like a shipmate and gave me a most gracious build-up, adding a pleasing "plug" for "Rig for Church."

Although I had with me what is called a "canned speech," I soon discarded it and spoke for thirty minutes the thoughts that fortunately came freely and appropriately. I recounted my experiences on the morning of December seventh and emphasized the paramount duties of a chaplain in battle. I spoke of the chaplain corps and its primary mission in the Navy. Finally I made a plea which has been the theme of many of my public addresses: to have confidence in our leaders in the line and the staff corps; to banish anxiety about their boys and to realize that they are in good hands. In brief, "Don't worry."

From the hotel, I was taken to radio station WJR for a broadcast. On the way I rehearsed a dialogue with the producer of the program, for there was no time to pre-

pare a script. At the studio, we immediately sat at a
table and began talking before a "mike." Still a bit
breathless, I was rushed to the Naval Reserve Armory
where Captain R. T. Brodhead, USNR, the senior naval
officer in the city, gave a Navy Day reception. I stood
in the receiving line for over an hour and shook hands
with hundreds of friends of the naval service. An amusing
incident made me quit feeling sorry for myself. The sister
of my old friend, Captain John Tom Bottom, presented
me with a pair of my own linen golf shorts which the
Chinese laundryman of Chefoo had in error delivered to
John ten years before. He had brought them home from
China intending to mail them to me and left them with
his thoughtful sister.

At ten that cold night, with Captain and Mrs. Brodhead, I attended a football game between teams representing Wayne University and Captain E. W. Litch's aviators. It marked for me the end of a long but exciting
scrimmage.

My orders directed me to remain an extra day and
address the Detroit Rotary Club luncheon. The next
morning we motored to the Chrysler tank arsenal where
we inspected the enormous plant. The Most Reverend
Edward Mooney, Archbishop of Detroit, joined the party.
We later put on dungarees and climbed aboard a tank
for a cold and rugged ride over terrain that had been
made scientifically bumpy. They placed me in the conn-
ing tower where I soon realized why there was ice in
the trenches and "shell craters" we bounded over. The
Archbishop rode in a lower compartment and, at the
end of the wild sortie, when he crawled out of the tank
with a broad grin on his face, he was covered with dust.
It was fun, but again I faced a "dead-line" and had to

hurry to the Hotel Statler to address the Detroit Rotarians.

My plans to return to San Diego were suddenly changed when telegraphic orders came to proceed to New York and broadcast the following Sunday on the Columbia Broadcasting System's "Church of the Air."

The Monday prologue, then Navy Day, followed by Wednesday's epilogue, comprised the most strenuous period in my naval career. It was a trilogy of days filled with large and small assignments in the public eye, and if the experience did nothing else, it made me feel sorry for those who live and work in the world's high places. I yearned for a billet in the fleet and the din of battle. If I had not realized the importance of my mission and if the members of the Navy Day Committee had been less kind and considerate, being lionized in a big city would have been extremely difficult to endure.

My friends took me to the train in the evening and expressed the hope that I might join them the following summer on a cruise of the Great Lakes. In June of 1943, still believing perhaps that I was free to move about the country at will, George Slocum in kindness sent me a telegram:

DEAR PADRE, COULD YOU ACCEPT INVITATION OF DETROIT BOARD OF COMMERCE TO GO ON ANNUAL CRUISE LEAVING HERE BY CHARTERED LAKE BOAT THURSDAY AFTERNOON JUNE 10TH RETURNING 8-00 MONDAY MORNING JUNE 14TH VISITING MACKINAC ISLAND AND LAKE CITIES IN INTEREST OF IMPROVING SUB CONTRACTORS WAR PLANT PRODUCTION CRUISE? YOUR PRESENCE WOULD BE GREATLY APPRECIATED BY YOUR MANY DETROIT FRIENDS.

With regret, I reminded my friend that even a Navy captain wearing a cross finds it just as difficult to leave his post as a city cop to wander from his beat.

CHAPTER XXV

I Meet the Governor

I MET MANY old friends on the night of my arrival in New York. My cousin, John P. Maguire, who then was regional director of the War Production Board in New York, gathered a group of men at the Union League Club for a dinner in my honor. It was quite typical of my distinguished kinsman who, for many years, has been my ideal as a Catholic gentleman. Whether as the head of an exemplary family, a true patriot, a successful business man, or a great friend, no one has proved more worthy of my admiration than he.

Among the guests who arrived conveniently early was ex-Governor Alfred Emanuel Smith. For several minutes, I sat between the Governor and my old friend Father Gerald C. Tracey, S. J., the President of Brooklyn Preparatory School. Father "Gerry" and I for many years have considered the Governor among the foremost American statesmen. I am sure my Jesuit friend was thrilled as much as I to be able to chat so informally with that famous patriot. I shall not attempt to name the two dozen or more men whom Jack had as guests. The Most Reverend Bishop Francis J. McIntyre came to represent His Excellency, Archbishop Francis J. Spellman. My old friend of Seton Hall days, Father Matthew J. Toohey, the chaplain of the Catholic War Veterans and pastor of St.

James Parish in Newark, New Jersey, sat next to me. John B. Kennedy, the writer and radio commentator, whom I have known for twenty years and my newly made friends, Lanny Ross, the singer, and Nick Kenny, the columnist, were there. All whom I have mentioned made brief speeches that stressed the mission of a chaplain in the armed forces. Nick Kenny told of his experiences as a bluejacket in the fleet and how his gang, the rather small men of the signal force of the battleship *Arizona* trained secretly and beat the ship's race boat crew "for their suits." Only Nick could have spun that yarn so well. Lanny Ross was in fine fettle and sang several entrancing numbers.

Jack Maguire, as toastmaster, kept things moving at a lively tempo. He was at his best on this occasion and he asked Governor Smith to speak at just the right moment. The beloved Al told a few stories before giving us his opinion on the state of the world at war. One of the stories I remember. It seems that a tourist arrived at a village and, being lonesome, decided to combine the job of filling the gas tank with a little conversation with the old man who ran the filling station. As the old timer picked up the gas hose the urbane traveller said, "I say, partner, what d'ya think of Hitler?"

"Never heard of him," was the reply.

"What's that? Never heard of him! What d'ya think of Mussolini?"

"Ain't heard of him neither," grunted the old timer.

"Don't you ever read the newspapers?"

"Naw, why should I read the papers?"

"Okay," said the salesman. "The heck with the gas— give me four new tires."

Inspired, perhaps, by what was said about the exalted

mission of the Army and Navy chaplain, John S. Burke, one of the guests, wrote a poem which someone, probably John B. Kennedy, read aloud:

> This is the sword of the spirit
> This is the Song of the Cross
> This is the Sign that shall win it
> Victory drawn from a loss.

The next day was Friday and the magazine *Life* carried my picture on the cover. In the lower left hand corner was the caption "Praise the Lord and Pass the Ammunition." The accompanying story clearly stated that I had not manned a gun at Pearl Harbor. But the sheet music was on the market carrying a story said to have been released by the Office of War Information and it told how I had left the altar to fire a gun at the Japs. This may have been the reason the Most Reverend Bishop John F. O'Hara, Military Vicar, held a press conference in his office on Saturday morning. Again I told the press that I had not performed as a combatant officer at Pearl Harbor and that I had no recollection of making up the popular war slogan. I explained it was not a proper occasion for speech-making and that I was too busy attending the wounded anyway. Bishop O'Hara said he wanted the press to get the truth of the matter as he feared the chaplains who were prisoners of the Japs might be placed in danger by the implications in the lyric of the song.

The military delegate, Archbishop Spellman, had me to luncheon that day and invited me to have breakfast with him after Mass on Sunday morning. John P. Maguire and his wife were also guests of the Archbishop at breakfast and they went with me to the studio for the broadcast on Columbia's "Church of the Air."

On Sunday afternoon, with a reservation on the "Century" to leave New York for San Diego, I was leaving the studio to pack my bag when I was told that a person in Buffalo, New York, was trying to reach me by telephone. He was one of the promoters of the "Armistice Day United Service of the Catholic, Jewish and Protestant Faiths," and he said arrangements were being made to have the Bureau of Naval Personnel order me to Buffalo to give the principal address at the Service. Again telegraphic orders arrived assigning me to temporary duty in New York City and to proceed to Buffalo in time for the Inter-Faith rally.

A telegram reached me via San Diego. It was sent by George F. Rand, Chairman of the United States Victory Fund Committee, regional group one. It read as follows:

ON BEHALF OF THE VICTORY FUND COMMITTEE AND THE WAR SAVINGS STAFF OF THE UNITED STATES TREASURY DEPARTMENT WE HAVE THE HONOR TO INVITE YOU TO BE THE PRINCIPAL SPEAKER AT A PATRIOTIC RELIGIOUS MASS MEETING TO BE HELD IN BUFFALO THE EVENING OF WEDNESDAY NOVEMBER ELEVENTH TO EMPHASIZE THE PLACE OF RELIGION IN OUR WAR EFFORT. MEETING IS SPONSORED BY ALL FAITHS AND ALL LOCAL CLERGYMEN. TREASURY DEPARTMENT NOW IN CONTACT WITH NAVY DEPARTMENT TO SECURE PERMISSION FOR YOUR ACCEPTANCE.

The Public Relations Office immediately booked me for various assignments on the radio and for making records of short speeches to be broadcast to the armed forces overseas.

There were a few idle hours given me during my active

week in New York. One evening I dined with Lanny Ross and his lovely wife in their apartment. While at dinner, we listened to John B. Kennedy's broadcast in which he spoke very kindly of me. Another evening, Jessica Dragonette, who was a school friend of my late sister Anita, invited a group of us to attend her broadcast on a coast-to-coast program. Jessica's voice that evening was still as captivating as the morning I first heard her sing as a little girl at a Mass which I offered in the college chapel.

I was fortunate in being in New York on the day "The Woman Pays Club" held the only luncheon of the year to which male guests are invited. The club is the counterpart of the famous "Dutch Treat Club" and the members are women who are self-supporting in the seven arts. I was the guest of Miss Nannine Joseph, one of the club's officers, and I was asked to make a little speech. I met many interesting and charming people on that occasion.

One day I made a hurried trip along the shore of the Hudson River to Newburgh, the birthplace of my mother, and visited relatives whom I had not seen for many years.

One afternoon, I motored to South Orange, New Jersey, to call on the Most Reverend Thomas J. Walsh, Archbishop of Newark. Jack Maguire came along and shared with me a very pleasant hour with the distinguished prelate.

The Archbishop spoke enthusiastically of his priests who were serving with the armed forces. He stressed the fact that he permitted only his most capable priests to become chaplains. It gave me a chance to tell His Excellency of the fine work Father George Shea was doing at the San Diego Training Station. Father Shea was a professor of dogmatic theology in the seminary when he volunteered to serve with the colors. I recently received a letter from him; it told of his labors with the Marines on one of the advance bases in the Solomons. It was most encouraging to hear the Archbishop proudly boast that the best of his young priests were serving as chaplains with our fighting men. It made me thankful to be one of his veteran chaplains.

This visit led to a day in New Jersey that was crammed full of activity. With Father Matthew Toohey as guide, I left New York in the morning and drove to Newark. As we passed through Jersey City, I reminisced about the year I spent as a curate in St. Mary's parish. Thoughts of those wonderful months when I was a young priest lingered a bit longer than I expected, as was evidenced when Father Matt introduced me to the children of his parish school. Forgetting that I had arrived in the heart of Newark, I told the youngsters how happy I was to be again in Jersey City whose people I so much admired. I wondered for a moment why they laughed.

From Newark we sped to the lovely town of South Orange where I addressed the children of Marylawn Academy. The students, dressed in their becoming uniforms, were not only attentive listeners but they were the sweetest youngsters I had seen in many a day. My cousin, Mary Francis Maguire, presented me to her fellow students and then I told them stories about the men of the Navy.

Our main objective that day was a visit to my alma mater, Seton Hall College. The President, the Rt. Rev. Monsignor James F. Kelley, had invited me to address the student body. After lunch in the faculty dining room, I was led to the auditorium of the new gymnasium where I found over a thousand students bursting with war spirit and anxious to hear what I had to say about Pearl Harbor and the Navy's job in World War II. They could not have done better by an old Setonian. My roommate at college, Father Walter A. Hennessy, was there and his presence made me feel quite at home.

My friends, the Ralph R. Huesmans of Los Angeles, were in New York at the time, and they invited me to join their party at the Notre Dame rally at the Waldorf on the eve of the football game with West Point. They and their guests occupied a box that gave a good view of the gay proceedings. Late in the evening, the master of ceremonies announced that I was present and he asked whether I would come to the stage and say a few words. It rather took my breath away but it was fun talking to friends of Notre Dame for they were in a very jovial mood. As a result of that impromptu performance, the university authorities asked the Bureau to permit me to stop off at South Bend and address the midshipmen.

The day before I left for Buffalo, Captain Frank Lowden of the Coast Guard took me across the bay to a camp where I spoke to a few hundred of his sailors. It was a fitting ending to a busy week.

CHAPTER XXVI

"He's a Notre Dame Man"

THE DAYLIGHT JOURNEY to Buffalo was made especially enjoyable by having as companions my cousin, John P. Maguire, and his secretary, Edward J. Cunningham. Jack chose this time to call a meeting of the War Production Board in Buffalo. It was certainly fine to have them along as I was beginning to feel the need of moral support.

The train arrived at five o'clock. On the station platform a committee of three churchmen extended a cordial greeting. They were the Rt. Rev. Cameron J. Davis, Episcopal Bishop of Western New York, Rabbi Joseph L. Fink, and the Rt. Rev. Monsignor Edmund J. Britt, Chancellor of the Buffalo Diocese. The Monsignor, a veteran chaplain of the First World War, was in the uniform of a captain of the New York Guard. The Catholic Bishop of Buffalo, the Most Rev. John A. Duffy, was in Washington attending the annual meeting of bishops. It was a keen disappointment not to see him. He was my favorite professor at Seton Hall when I was a student there in 1909. Monsignor Britt invited me to stay at the cathedral rectory, an old, homey sort of a place. A few moments after we arrived, I again faced the reporters, gave them an interview, climbed into my overcoat, and again set forth, this time to dine as a guest of the officers of a State Guard regiment. Another speech. After dinner we motored to an armory where Major General William Ottman, Commander of the State Guard, who had come from New York that day, asked me to accompany him while he inspected the troops. The 74th Regiment staged a smart show that evening. The soldiers were well trained and their spirit was excellent.

In the afternoon of Armistice Day, I addressed a group of men who had recently enlisted in the Navy. They were assembled in a large room of the Post Office building. I gave them a verbal pat on the back and wished them God-speed.

Before going to Kleinhans Music Hall where the United Service was to be held, Monsignor Britt and I had dinner with members of the committee in charge. I sat at a table with Bishop and Mrs. Davis and discovered, in the course of our conversation, that Major Harold Jones of the Marine Corps, whom I had met in Hawaii, was their son-in-law.

In spite of a heavy snow-storm, nearly three thousand people came to the Music Hall; they read on the cover of the program the following statement:

> "In dedication of ourselves and our
> substance to those spiritual ideals at
> stake in the war."

Bishop Davis presided; several ministers spoke briefly and Rabbi Fink spoke for the Jews. Monsignor Britt read a letter from Bishop John Duffy which he had specially written for that important occasion.

I considered it a high privilege to take part in Buffalo's religious and patriotic service. It marked a step forward from the undignified and frivolous appeal to buy war bonds which had previously been made throughout the country. I expressed, in the course of my address, the hope that other cities would follow the lead of Buffalo and give the people a religious motive in their effort to finance the total war. The audience, at the close of the service, pledged themselves to buy war bonds to the amount of $800,000.

At midnight I boarded a train for South Bend, Indiana, thrilled with the prospect of meeting the faculty and students of Notre Dame. As I told the New York alumni at the football rally, I felt like the fighting Irishman, who, though he had not gotten out of the eighth grade, was proud to call Notre Dame his alma mater. My brother Walter was graduated as a mechanical engineer in 1912. His stories of the days when the immortal Knute Rockne played football there aroused my interest. My friend of the Catholic University days, Lucien B. Coppinger, had spent a few years as a student there and he often regaled me with a word picture of the life and spirit of Notre Dame. My experience with the graduates whom I met in the Service has proved to me that the university turns out an excellent type of Christian gentleman.

My friend and *Idaho* shipmate, Captain Henry P. "Bobbie" Burnett and his wife, met me at the station. The Captain was in command of the naval unit of a thousand or more midshipmen who were in training for commissions as sea-going officers of the Naval Reserve. The Burnetts took me to their home and gave me the lay of the land. We had a good talk about old times and old friends. I then told them I would like to pay my respects to the Reverend Sister M. Madeleva, the President of St. Mary's College, which was not far from the Notre Dame campus. I had read her exquisite poetry and heard so much about her good works from our mutual friends that I dreaded missing this chance to meet her. J. Arthur Haley, Director of Public Relations on the university staff, drove me to St. Mary's and I met the famous President. We chatted for a few minutes, and then came the inevitable: Sister Madeleva asked me to address the nuns and students of the college.

At dinner that evening at which the Vice President, the Reverend John C. Cavanaugh, C.S.C., presided, I met many of the trustees who had come to the university to attend their annual meeting which, I believe, may have seemed to some less important than attending the Michigan game the following Saturday. Everyone talked about the game and wondered how I could be so prosaic as to by-pass it. I explained that my orders called for immediate departure after addressing the midshipmen, but Captain Burnett came to my rescue and said that inasmuch as I had reported to him for duty, he would hold me in his command until after the game.

That evening, I spoke to over four thousand midshipmen and university students and enjoyed the experience immensely. I talked for forty minutes, and not a soul went to sleep.

Perhaps the most interesting experience I enjoyed at Notre Dame was the football rally of the Fighting Irish the night before the game. Frank Leahy, head coach, Clarence Manion, dean of the Law School, and Harry "Red" Miller, captain of the team which had beaten Michigan thirty years before and whose two sons were playing on the first team, and Father John McGinn, the popular professor, gave pep talks that brought the gay students to their toes. Then they led me to the "mike" while the band played "Praise the Lord and Pass the

Ammunition." As a punch line at the end, I said, "Fellows, I have a new one for you. 'Praise the Lord and make it tough for Michigan.' " A cheer leader jumped to his feet and shouted, "He's a Notre Dame man." Then all hands gave the famous cheer:

"He's a man!
Who's a man?
He's a Notre Dame man!
Chaplain Maguire
Chaplain Maguire
Chaplain Maguire
Rah! Rah! Rah!"

I was thereby elected an honorary Notre Dame man, and it made me feel good.

On the morning of the game, Ray Miller, whom I had first met in Brest, in the summer of 1918, took me on a search for Father Walsh, a former Army chaplain who was with Ray the night I had them both to dinner at the naval officers' mess. We failed to find him. We then motored to the country home of Dean and Mrs. Manion where we enjoyed an hour of delightful hospitality.

The president of the university, the Reverend J. Hugh O'Donnell, C.S.C., invited me to see the game, seated beside him in the presidential box. It quickly became evident that Father O'Donnell understood the science of football and he revealed superb sportsmanship as he witnessed a Notre Dame defeat in a hard and cleanly fought battle on the gridiron. I dined that evening in the home of Arthur Haley and his wife.

Notre Dame fulfilled my highest expectations. I felt I had caught something of the spirit of that famous font of Catholic culture. On Sunday, when I boarded the train for California, I felt I had taken on a new responsibility, that of being "a Notre Dame man."

I disembarked at Pasadena and spoke that afternoon to the students of the Flintridge Sacred Heart Academy which is run by the Dominican nuns. Anita Nolan, my niece, entered as a student there in 1937 and I have shared her enthusiasm and her affection for that splendid school for girls.

It all started with Navy Day in Detroit, but the long grind of speech-making, though trying, was worthwhile. I returned to the naval training station with the satisfaction of having given to the parents of the American bluejacket a message of comfort and encouragement. I have felt, since the outbreak of war, that the "will to win" which we try to engender in the hearts of our young sailors depends a great deal on the attitude of their parents. From the letters many people sent me, I learned that on the home-front there is need of reminding our citizens that sacrifices and sufferings are to be expected in war time and that they should have confidence in our civil and military leaders.

A few days after my return to San Diego, I attended the monthly meeting of Army and Navy chaplains and diocesan auxiliary chaplains which the Most Reverend Charles F. Buddy, Bishop of San Diego, held at his residence. Our great friend and spiritual leader started the proceedings with a fine dinner and we then discussed the many problems that come up in our work with the armed forces. The monthly meetings were not only a delightful experience but they lifted our spirits and renewed our zeal. Bishop Buddy will never know the extent of his influence on the work of the service chaplains who have had the good fortune to profit by his leadership and sound counsel. As a militant shepherd of souls, he is our champion and great friend. I have known His Excellency since the day of his installation as Bishop of San Diego, and I am proud that he is the vicar delegate in this area.

In November, the Most Reverend John J. Mitty, D.D., Archbishop of San Francisco, invited me to offer a Solemn Military Mass of Requiem in St. Mary's Cathedral for the late Rear Admiral Daniel J. Callaghan. The following week, the Archbishop again invited me to San Francisco to preach at a Solemn Military Mass in commemoration of Pearl Harbor Day. In announcing the Mass, His Excellency said, "The Mass will be offered to commemorate the sacrifices at Pearl Harbor and to honor our heroes who there gave their lives, to beg God's blessing upon all our armed forces, and to pray for victory and peace pleasing to His divine will." I felt especially honored to be the guest of the great American prelate whom I first met as an Army chaplain in 1918, standing in the mud of Pontenezen Barracks near Brest. It was the day he left to join his regiment at the front.

I shall always regret that the exigencies of the service did not permit me to make another speaking tour in January, 1943. First came an invitation from the Reverend John A. Cashen, Rector of Our Lady of the Rosary Cathedral, to speak to three thousand people of Duluth, Minnesota. The Carroll Club of New York invited me to address three thousand women at their annual Communion breakfast. Catholic Charities, Inc., of Altoona, Pennsylvania, hoped that I might also address them in the interest of war effort. And to complete the circuit, Lucien B.

Coppinger, President of the Pennsylvania Shipyards, Inc. of Beaumont, Texas, asked that I address his eight thousand workers for the purpose of defeating the evil of absenteeism. It was difficult to convince my friends that my eastern activities in the autumn of 1942 were directed entirely by official orders from Washington and not the result of "accepting" invitations.

CHAPTER XXVII

On to Victory

WRITING THIS SEQUEL to "Rig for Church" involved what the bluejackets call "extra duty." Now that it is published, my friends will know why, for the past six months, I have spent so many evenings alone in the seclusion of my hill-top home. Some may wonder why I took the time to write such a book, and my answer is that I hoped to add information of value regarding the life of a Navy chaplain, and the nature of his work among officers and men of the service. I thought it might serve as an entertaining guide for young churchmen who some day may be on the quest for a missionary life of extraordinary possibilities. The Navy is such a missionary field. If this book succeeds in recruiting one good chaplain for the Navy, I shall be well repaid for the "extra duty" the writing of it demanded.

It was tempting, as I approached the hour for sounding taps on this extra-curricular enterprise, to bring "Rig for Church" up to date by telling what became of the officers and men who were mentioned in that brief autobiography. It was to be expected that I should hear from my boyhood playmates of Paterson, New Jersey. When I was in New York in the fall of 1942, I spoke with John Grimshaw on the telephone. Fred Neuburger, Lionel Reed and Jim Kearns, all successful business men, have frequently written to me. Lee "Red" Durbin, my yeoman in Hawaii, is now a chief yeoman, serving in the office of the Commander Destroyers Pacific Fleet. Joe Workman, "Red's" assistant, is serving in a big transport. He recently wired me from San Francisco.

The heroine of the chapter, "The Army Nurse," who is now Mrs. S. E. Smith, one day wrote from Florida. After twenty-four years wondering what had become of her, I received this letter:

I've been thinking of writing to you ever since I heard you talk on Nelson Eddy's program. I was serving while I listened and when I realized it was you talking, I was very much moved. . . . Just after I heard your broadcast, I visited in North Carolina, and my brother Jack, the one you sent for when I was sick (in France), showed me a copy of a Catholic magazine called *Pax* which had an extract from your book "Rig for Church;" it was "The Army Nurse." I can't tell you how I felt that you remembered me, and how humble, at the things you said. I am married now and have had five children. I lost one little boy nearly six years ago. My oldest is a girl nearly sixteen; she is a junior in high school. They all go to our Catholic school here, two boys and two girls. My back still gives me trouble, otherwise I am very well. . . . You are probably on the other side of the world but I am going to hope that you get this and let me hear from you. I have never ceased to be grateful to you for being so good to me when I was sick, so far away from home. . . .

Whenever I see an Army nurse, I invariably recall how Miss Rosetta Shannon, the frail little red-head, although she too was sick, volunteered to attend the dying soldiers in the Pontenezen Hospital near Brest. They were victims of spinal meningitis. Rosetta served them until she too was stricken with that dread disease, and came close to death. Her magnificent deed of self-sacrifice in the awful quiet of that hospital ward was the most heroic act I have ever witnessed.

To have survived the vicissitudes of twenty-six years of an active life in the Navy, sixteen of which were spent in all parts of the world, calling a steel locker my home, has made me truly grateful. When I learned that T. Mahlon "Tip" Tisdale, whom I first knew as a young, handsome flag lieutenant in Brest, is now a vice admiral in command of a large force of fighting ships in the Pacific, it increased my regard for the Naval Academy and for the service Tip loves. He and I were shipmates in the middle twenties when he was executive officer of the old *Aroostook*, a seaplane tender, which we fondly called the "Beeno." Tip showed every sign in those days that he was destined for high command. I am grateful that he was chosen to lead our sea forces in this hour of national peril.

My old shipmates of the formative period of naval aviation have important commands in the war zone. They now are admirals and captains. James E. Dyer, who, twenty years ago was a young fighter pilot and a shipmate, is now commanding Naval Operating Base, Kodiak, Alaska. I last saw my friend Jim when he was returning from the Philippines in 1941. He came to Honolulu by clipper and spent a few days with me. During the past year, I have frequently dined in the Dyer home with his wife Eva and little Ann. It is only through conversation that the whereabouts of one's friends become known these war days, for orders are no longer published. It is especially comforting to learn that your old friends whom you have known and served with in the fleet are at last in positions of great responsibility, that they are in command of large groups of fighting men, leading them through battle to victory.

In "Rig for Church," I frequently mentioned the distinguished officer who generously wrote a foreword, my dear friend G. Barry Wilson. He is now a rear admiral and he writes to me from overseas where he holds an extremely important position.

A few weeks ago I addressed the students of Brown Military Academy at San Diego. Just before leaving to return to my office, I chatted with a young cadet who is the son of Lewis Merritt with whom I served when he was a young captain in the U. S. Marine Corps. I ran across Lewie a few days ago and had the pleasure of addressing him as "General." He is in command of a large unit of aviators. We spoke of the hop he once gave me in his dive bomber over the volcano of Mauna Loa in Hawaii.

Perhaps the most important assignment I had in the spring of 1943 was a fifteen-minute broadcast on the National Catholic Hour on Memorial Day. The Right Reverend Monsignor Michael Ready, Executive Secretary of the National Catholic Welfare Conference, invited me to give the first of a series of six talks by Catholic Army and Navy chaplains who were stationed at home, in North Africa and the southwest Pacific.

It was the second time I had thus been honored. The series was called "A Second Report to Mothers and Fathers." The Catholic Hour, which was started more than thirteen years ago in cooperation with the National Broadcasting Company, reaches an enormous listening public over eighty-nine stations. More than 130,000 letters from the radio audience were received last year.

My fellow Navy chaplains, Father John F. Robinson, who is a member of the faculty of the Chaplain's School at Williamsburg, Virginia, and Father John R. Boslet attached to the office of the Chief of Chaplains, later spoke from Washington.

I gave the broadcast from the N.B.C. studio in Hollywood. It seems fitting that I incorporate in this book what I said on that day to millions of fellow Americans. This is part of the talk on the Catholic Hour.

"Memorial Day of 1943 might well be called a day of humble thanksgiving. Are we not convinced of the sterling courage and strength of the youth who now serve with the colors? Are we not satisfied that the Axis powers were mistaken when they thought that our ideal of a peaceful, charitable way of life had weakened the sinews of our manhood? At Pearl Harbor, on that fateful December seventh, my duties gave me the privilege of learning how unmistakably our American homes had reared an heroic brood of fighting men. You have heard how our soldiers, sailors and Marines overcame the handicap of treacherous surprise and fought the enemy with skill and valor. On that Sunday morning, the names of a thousand martyrs joined the honored scroll of truly patriotic men.

"This dreadful war has placed millions of blue stars on the banners of the American family. But among those stars are many that are gold, and though they tell us a story of bereavement and sorrow, they remind us of the precious sacrifice of the heroes they honor and the spirit of the people who have gold stars to display. There is not a gold star in the land that does not attest that he for whom it stands gave his life willingly and manfully as an earnest of his love for his home and his family, and his conviction that, 'Greater love than this no man hath, that a man lay down his life for his friends.' (*John* 15:13).

"During the twelve months that have passed, the universal war effort of the American people has borne abundant fruit. In every section of the land we find our citizens responding with heart and soul to the call to arms. In every machine shop, factory and mill, men and women are showing that they know what it means when hundreds of thousands of American boys and girls, unaided by the stimulus of flag-waving and martial music, grimly put to sea with a course set toward the enemy's lair, and with one purpose—to fight him wherever they find him. This is not a singing war—it is a fighting war. During the past year, our men and their comrades of the United Nations have won many hard-earned victories.

"I knew the Pearl Harbor bluejacket, for I met him the day he came in sports clothes to the gate of our training station. Then, for four years, I served with him in ships of the Pacific Fleet, observing him at drills, in sea maneuvers and on liberty ashore. I greeted him on board ship when he came to worship God at Holy Mass. His heroic performance at Pearl Harbor did not surprise me. He joined the Navy, fired with the free spirit of the American boy, cheerfully ready to face a period of mental and physical training which changed him from a happy-go-lucky immature lad, into a dependable, efficient, God-fearing man of the sea. The change was not a difficult process because he had already learned in his Christian home of the ideals of citizenship. He also knew that the Navy was not a national instrument of aggression but a first line of defense of a nation which had taught him that it is a God-given right to be free to live peacefully in the pursuit of happiness, and that it is a sacred duty to recognize that our fellow men are entitled to that same right.

"It is gratifying to know that it is not necessary, in the Nazi and Nipponese manner, to brutalize our young men in order to fit them to fight a ruthless enemy. Those of our heroes who have already returned from the scene of battle are little changed except for the claims of wounds and sickness. They may be concerned about conditions on the home-front but they feel out there that they and their comrades are taking part in a modern crusade. Their aim in this fight for freedom is to do their duty without fear and without reproach.

"We can be thankful for the way the American people have answered the Axis threats to destroy our freedom. Every home in the land has its representatives doing their share of the work to save us from ruin. Every home in the land is suffering the shock of this war's unlimited demands because our women, faced as they are with new tasks and strange responsibilities, are now called upon reluctantly to take a more active part in the war effort while at the same time they must preserve their sanctified place of responsibility in the home which is the center of love and beauty and all that is fine.

"The men of our armed forces are well equipped to fulfill their mission and their letters to you tell of the thoroughness of their training for battle. As never before, our military and naval leaders are selecting officers and men for placement under training for which they are best fitted. For the past twelve months I have noticed an absence of hurry and nervousness in the way the work is being done. The rapid expansion in personnel and material that marked the early days of the war, has given way to a steady, cool and studious procedure. Our men receive the best of food; they are comfortably housed; welfare officers provide athletics and other forms of amusement; doctors and nurses care for them in excellent hospitals; in new chapels ashore and on the decks of our ships at sea, churchmen serve in their apostolate the precious souls of our fighting men.

"From the point of view which years of naval experience have given me, I feel impelled to ask you, my friends of the Catholic Hour, not to worry about your boys. The American sailor or Marine leads an ordered life; he works through a disciplined day; he is inspired by ideals and traditions of an honorable service; his spiritual needs are recognized and they receive careful attention. After twenty-six years in the Chaplain Corps of the Navy, I have enjoyed many happy compensations, and not the least has been the privilege of standing before large groups of strong men; to call for a volunteer to serve at Holy Mass and to find a husky bosun's mate step up and become again a bashful altar boy. The Mass and the Sacraments really matter in the life of our soldier, bluejacket and Marine.

"One of the strange paradoxes of this dreadful war is that even while men go forth on orders to kill, they meet God as they go. Perhaps they recall the words of our Savior, 'Render therefore to Caesar the things that are Caesar's; and to God, the things that are God's.' (*Matthew* 22:21).

"We priests are not worried about your boy. You gave him a good start when he was young. You taught him how to pray and how to respect and revere his Church and how to live in the way of Christ's teaching. You made of him a good citizen and a true patriot.

"If you could hear your son sing at Mass the hymns he used to sing in his church back home, such favorites as, 'Mother Dear O Pray For Me' and 'Holy God We Praise Thy Name,' you would have less anxiety in your heart, for you are greatly responsible for his Faith and his strong and good character. As evidence of what the Church has given your boy, here is a quotation from a letter written to his parents by a young paratrooper Marine in the South Pacific.* 'During the week you seem so far away and then during Mass on Sunday, I seem to be so close to you that when Mass is over, I turn around to look at you —to walk home with you.' We priests are merely taking over the duties you so well performed when your boy sought comfort and guidance from your maternal heart.

"To the mothers, wives and sweethearts whose loved ones no longer live to bear the brunt of battle, may God in His mercy lessen the burden of your sorrow.

"To you whose sons, daughters and husbands are still carrying on the hard fight, may I again say, 'Do not worry. Pray for them with full resignation to God's will. Write often to them but always cheerfully. You have been told this before but it is really quite important that you show that you also are brave by keeping from your letters all trivial troubles of the home lest you cause your valiant men to worry about you.'

"Today we can be thankful for the progress we are making. God grant that next year, Memorial Day may dawn in the glow of triumphant peace."

In the spring of 1943 it was often my good fortune to have in my home young chaplains lately arrived from the scene of battle. The first to come from the Southwest Pacific was Father Arthur F. McQuaid who was on board a heavy cruiser the night one of our task forces fought a night engagement with the Japs in the Solomons. He was badly burned when a torpedo struck near the bow of the ship; sheets of flame burned him almost fatally as

* John Hayes of La Mesa, California.

he stood at his battle station on the signal bridge. He was, however, in excellent spirits and he expressed the hope he might return to his ship when fully recovered.

Chaplain Frank R. Hamilton, who was on the carrier *Yorktown*, when she was sunk in the Midway battle, arrived with orders to the training station. Frank, fortunately, survived the ordeal, hale and hearty. His story of the battle complemented the account Father John Wolach gave me when he came through San Diego on his way to the East coast. Father John saw the battle from a dugout on the Island. He spoke highly of the work of Commander John Ford who took motion pictures under fire, and of the performance of Lieutenant D. Judson Callaghan, the son of the late Rear Admiral Callaghan. Jud fought the battle in a PT boat.

The most vivid account of the fighting on Guadalcanal I have yet heard was told by Father Matthew F. Keough who served with the Marines all through the campaign. I invited him one day to the training station and had him tell the junior chaplains of his thrilling experiences. His lecture followed soon after the talk given us by Father Charles J. Hacherl of the regular Navy who was at that time chaplain of a battleship. Father Charley is an old friend and one of the outstanding chaplains of the younger generation. As an amateur chef he stands No. 1 in the opinion of my popular colored house-keeper, Mrs. Katherine Shakespeare. Katherine has made it known to me that Father Charley's chicken stew *mit strudels* is "tops." He is now the chaplain of our newest first-line carrier, and it is a safe bet the smiling padre is the best liked member of the ship's company.

It was a great pleasure to be invited by my old friend the Right Reverend Monsignor Bernard J. Dolan to

address the Rotary Club of Long Beach, California in
July, 1943. The Monsignor is a staunch friend of the
Navy.

Early in July I heard the voice on the telephone of my
old friend, Father Joseph P. Mannion. He is now a quali-
fied Marine paratrooper and is with a regiment which is
undergoing advanced training in California. Father Joe
is just the man for such a tough job.

In May, 1943, the officers and men of the Naval Training Station, especially the old timers, witnessed one of the
more pleasing aspects of fighting a global war. I cannot
say they were shocked but they certainly were amazed
when over a hundred young women, dressed in Navy blue,
with rating badges on their arms, joined the ship's company as WAVES. My first impression was, "What a
lovely decorative addition to our beautiful station," for
they really were charming. But it did not take long to
realize that we happily had acquired a group of shipmates
who were fully indoctrinated in Navy ways; but what is
more important they were willing and able to pull their
weight in the boat with the rest of us.

I have read much about the WACS, MARINES and
SPARS. I have visited war plants where seventy per cent
of the personnel were hard-working women, but at the
training station, I see in daily action the WAVES whose
coming has released a hundred able-bodied men for duty
in our ships of the fighting fleet.

Many letters have come to me from anxious parents who
ask whether their daughters in the WAVES are in danger
of the rocks and shoals of Navy life. In my replies, I mention the fine leadership of the highly trained corps of
commissioned officers in these organizations of service
women, and I remind them that the daily routine of service

with the colors, motivated by love of God and country, is good for the soul.

It is not expected that the women of the armed forces in their free time should remain always on the station or in the barracks, where all they are apt to hear is shop talk, scuttlebutt and careless griping. It is so much better that they occasionally "get away from it all," go to town to a place like the USO for the stimulating tonic of music, dancing and a few good laughs. The Navy calls it "going on liberty," going somewhere with friends far from the job, in free quest of renewed enthusiasm for the task of waging a global war. The women of the armed forces, serving in the San Diego area, have a large USO club house and it is a favorite rendezvous of the WAVES. I gave a short radio address there the day the club was opened.

I recently organized on the training station a "Stella Maris Sodality" made up of thirty or more Catholic WAVES. On Monday, after office hours, they come as a group to evening Mass in the chapel of Mary Star of the Sea. The WAVES of the Protestant Faith are showing their interest in the religious activities of the station by joining the station choir. We are proud of Lieutenant (jg) Vesta Wiley's woman bluejackets.

Although the Navy has lately grown to unbelievable size and strength which has required the induction of hastily trained officers and men, it is my hope that the type of naval officer who received his early training at Annapolis will prevail. The Naval Academy graduates and the officers who are like them, as they mature with sea experience, become throughout the world, ambassadors of good will. The Navy, as I have known and loved it, has

Annapolis to thank for the splendid traditions her sons
have kept alive dutifully and with dignity.

In the Navy, God willing, I will go on to victory.

You never know in the Navy what may turn up. The
following may seem fictional but it really happened. A
few minutes after I told my friend and shipmate, Lyle
Johnson, my yeoman, who, in his off time typed the pages
of this book, "Lyle, there it is. Pull the old zipper. That's
the end," the 'phone rang. It was Major General Holland
McT. Smith, Commanding General Amphibious Corps,
Pacific Fleet. He said, "You are to receive orders to serve
on my staff. I hope the orders come soon because we're
going places." It took my breath away. I had become
reconciled to a future "on the beach." During World War
I, I tried hard to join the Marines. The prospect of serving
with General Smith and his aide, Lieutenant Colonel Peter
P. Schrider, the aviator, and to be a padre for the fighting
leathernecks, made my heart jump for joy.

Please, my friend, say a prayer that we may speed the
winning of blessed peace.

Index